Vestiges
of
Memory

By
Sid Winter

COMTEQ
PUBLISHING
MARGATE, NEW JERSEY

Published by:
  ComteQ Publishing
  A division of ComteQ Communications, LLC
  101 N. Washington Ave. • Suite 2B
  Margate, New Jersey 08402
  609-487-9000 • Fax 609-487-9099
  Email: publisher@ComteQpublishing.com
  Website: www.ComteQpublishing.com

ISBN 978-1-935232-29-2
Library of Congress Control Number: 2010937950

Cover design by Rob Huberman

Printed in the United States of America
10 9 8 7 6 5 4 3 2 1

Dedicated to my parents,
Becky and Sam Winter

"A journey of a thousand miles must begin with a single step"
Lao-Tzu Circa 604 BC – Circa 531 BC

Acknowledgments

I would like to thank the following people who helped me make this work, 'Vestiges of Memory' come to fruition. My daughter and son-in-law Sabrina and Robert Denmark and my son Mark Winter for their valuable criticisms and editing skills. My daughter Jennifer McNulty and my sister Helen Wechsler for their encouragement. Judy Klein for her unbiased commentaries and tolerance serving as a sounding board concerning the working of this manuscript. My close friends Judy Kabus and especially Irwin Kabus who listened, read and critiqued my work. I would further thank Don Bloom for his artistic illustrations and valuable insights in this project.

I would especially like to thank Perry Montauredes of Black Horse Studios for his talented contributions concerning the sound effects and recording of this work.

Together as a family of friends and relatives I am indebted to them all for their worthy input and major contributions in producing this labor of love entitled, 'Vestiges of Memory'.

I would also like to thank Rutgers University Library's Alexander Archivel reference branch in New Brunswick, New Jersey, the East Brunswick Public Library and the Franklin Township Public Library in Somerset, New Jersey for the use of their facilities and informational guidance in this project.

Table of Contents

Prologue 9

Book I

The Ice Cream Man 13
The Chicken Man 23
The Fireman 37
The Letter 47
The Chair 53
The Dish 73

Book II

The Cloud 95
Becky's Boy 101
Sam's Son 121
The Glove 141
The Jacket 147
Walking 167
Either Something, Either Nothing 177
Epilogue 182

Prologue

In the most horrific physical tragedies, earthquakes, volcanic eruptions, hurricanes, forest fires, floods or tsunamis, people en masse scurry for their lives. They gather whatever material possessions they can take with them when they flee. Invariably they take jewelry, cash and, most valuable of all, photographs and family memorabilia.

Prisoners of war don't have that option, but many who survive mentally sustain themselves by remembering and reliving their past experiences with loved ones. These reminiscences are their life's blood.

I believe that the spirit and soul of a person lies in anecdotes and remembrances. When a person passes on, we should not be so concerned with inheriting bank accounts, securities and real estate but rather with recalling the words and deeds of the individual.

Memories are the finest record we have of people—a permanent legacy that can live in posterity when handed down from one generation to another.

A grave marking identifies someone in only a cursory way. Beyond photographs lies the essence of a person.

In *Vestiges of Memory,* I have tapped the wordsmith and voice within to recapture significant experiences of my life and to bare my soul and lie naked before all to see. It is my hope that I adequately expressed these episodic moments of my childhood travails and accomplishments and ensured the reader's ability to relate them to their own lives.

Coming from humble beginnings, I firmly believe that one need not achieve the status of war hero, celebrity, politician or millionaire to be worthy of being depicted in an autobiographical format.

Let us look with a discerning eye, witness and hear again in our minds the meaningful memories and reminiscences of common folk—who like me, may turn out not to be so common after all.

BOOK ONE

The Ice Cream Man

Before I could read or write or went to school, before I had any friends my age, or even before I knew the meaning and value of money I heard the bells. The soft little bells ringing gently on Joe's ice cream truck as he came by my house on that first warm, spring like day.

This is where he parked his vehicle under the street light beside the house where I lived. It happened regularly, three or four times a day, as if preordained, usually at the same time in the same setting.

I would look out my window and gaze at the kids on the block running as swiftly as strong winter winds towards what they perceived as nirvana. Sometimes they went by themselves, and other times with their parents. They would line up and either speak to Joe directly, telling him what they wanted, or point to a picture logo pasted on the colorful white ice-cream wagon. I looked in wonderment as Joe opened various small compartment doors and pulled out packages, like a magician, to fulfill their unique desires as their eyes twinkled with joyous appreciation and acknowledgement.

Although being sickly, introverted, fearful and reclusive as a pre-school child, I asked my mother (quite out of character for me) if I could go out at that moment. She was overwhelmed and happy to get rid of me for a few moments and said, "Ok, but stay by the house."

What could be better? I could see Joe, his truck, watch the other kids, see what all the fuss was about and still be by my house.

"Put your jacket on, not to catch a cold," she said loudly to me in Yiddish, her first and only language.

I was thrilled, this being my first real adventure into the real world by myself. By the time I got out of the house, Joe was gone. And so was everyone else. I was greatly disappointed. However, the saving grace would always be that Joe would eventually return. But when?

I vowed that the next time he arrived I would be ready. The next day came and passed with no Joe. I was sad, moody and despondent as an impulsive child would be, not understanding why Joe didn't appear.

A day later I heard the bells from the distance beyond where I lived. Like one of Pavlov's dogs, I began to salivate in anticipation of Joe's arrival. This time I ran to my mother and demanded that I wanted to go out.

She was shocked at my aggressive demeanor.

I went to the closet and got my jacket, hat and gloves so as not to be late, and ran out the door, not listening to my mother saying, "Stay by the house."

There I was, the first one in line, looking at Joe as if he were a god. "What do you want?" he asked nicely.

I answered, "Where were you yesterday?"

He answered, "It was raining; too hard to go out."

I now understood why he was not there the day before.

By now there were many kids by the truck. I got off the line, turned around and stood by the sidewalk, watching while the other kids gave Joe money after they selected their choice of ice cream. Joe gave them their favorite ice cream in a package. Then, in a magical way, Joe would take their money and give them change from a silver looking change maker. I was astonished.

My eyes fixed on the change maker and the quick clicking of his finger. The doors he opened were small refrigerator freezers built into the truck with handles on the outside that housed the ice cream which he quickly opened and closed tightly.

I marveled at the fact that there were so many doors and that Joe could immediately reach in and pull out the exact item the kid requested. When the kids opened the packages they all started eating different kinds of ice cream. I was mesmerized, watching and taking it all in.

After all the kids left I was still standing there on the sidewalk, almost in a trance. Joe approached me hiding his hand behind his back, and like pulling a rabbit out of a hat, produced a package on a stick and gave it to me.

"This is for you little boy," he said. It was a chocolate coated vanilla ice cream pop.

This was the first time anyone, besides my parents, had ever given me anything. I was speechless. He smiled and said, "Eat it or it will all melt." I obliged, as this was my first ice cream ever. I ate every morsel and licked the pop stick. I ran into my house and my mother noticed there were ice cream smudges on my face.

She asked me, "Where did you get what you just ate?"

I didn't want to tell. I was frightened and excited at the same time. She persisted, rapidly firing multiple questions at me. "What were you eating, who gave it to you? Didn't I tell you not to take anything from anybody you didn't know. How could you do such a thing?"

I cried and softly said, "The ice cream man…"

"We don't take charity from anybody. If you want something, anything, you ask me. Next time he comes I want to talk to him, understand?"

I felt awful and confused. I felt like a rat being unfaithful to Joe. I didn't know what my mother's response to Joe would be, when or if they would ever meet. Would there be a confrontation, a fight, who knows what… I wondered to myself. This was the first major crisis in my life. How would it be resolved?

The next day I heard the little soft sound of the bells, but I was too frightened and fearful to get my mother. I didn't have the confidence within myself to pursue the matter further. That night, I tossed and turned in an attempt to sleep soundly, but I could not. I came to the conclusion that the only way to resolve my dilemma was to meet the problem directly. My mind was made up. The next day when Joe came, I would get my mother.

As predictable as a morning sunrise, I heard the bells, ran towards my mother, pulled on her skirt and said, "Joe's here, let's go or he will be gone."

"Alright, alright," she answered quickly. She put on a jacket to cover her cleaning clothes and then grabbed her little purse in a gruff manner. My mother, Becky Winter, was a fastidious cleaner. It's the one thing she did best. Our house was always spotless, never a crumb to be found, never a dish in the sink.

Everything was always in the same place. The living room's soft furniture was covered in plastic. The wood furniture was covered over with towels to protect it from the sun and house dust. Our home was immaculate. I was afraid of making a mess or bringing any kind of dirt into the house. My mother's aggressive mood seemed to match her fierce temper.

I was scared about the upcoming confrontation with Joe. One thing was for sure, I would be in the center of what would be happening next. I would be the eye witness. My anticipation was killing me. I just couldn't wait any longer.

Joe was always dressed in white with a white hat to match his uniform. He was short, had a dark, Mediterranean complexion, as if sunburned to go with his dark black hair and little potbelly. He had a distinguished pencil thin mustache accentuating his image as the ice cream man with the change maker attached to his belt.

No two people who were to meet each other were more different. The only thing they had in common was their heavy accent when they spoke. My mother's was Yiddish, Joe's was Italian.

I was my mother's translator. She asked me to ask Joe why he gave me the ice cream pop the other day.

He explained, "Your son seemed sad because the other kids got ice cream and that he wanted what they had gotten but he didn't have any money. That's why I gave him the pop."

My mother respectfully acknowledged his kindness and asked how much the ice cream cost. She said, with pride, that I should tell him that we don't want anything for nothing and gave him a folded up dollar.

He said, "I couldn't take money for what I gave him as a present, but if your son wants something now, I would accept the money." She agreed. They both smiled. Joe pointed at the ice cream decals.

I said, "Give me what you gave me before." Joe thought for a moment, remembered and pulled out an ice cream pop. I smiled. Joe clicked away like crazy and gave my mother ninety-five cents change. Watching him was almost as good as the ice cream itself.

My mother was impressed and pleased. She now knew the cost of the item and saw that Joe was honest and could be trusted to take care of me. Then Joe asked me what my name was. My mother answered, "Moisha."

Joe had trouble with the pronunciation and settled for "Moish." He was the only person who ever called me Moish. Joe then pointed to the pop on the stick and said it might be a lucky pop. I didn't understand.

He explained that some pops were lucky in that they had markings on the stick which entitled the owner to a free ice cream. Apparently he knew that the pop he gave me was a lucky pop. After I finished eating the pop I saw the marking. This day turned into a happy occasion for all concerned.

However, with the passage of time, a stranger came riding

down the block on a three wheel, white bicycle ice cream wagon, carrying a new brand of ice cream. This was my first contact with "The Good Humor Man." It was Eskimo Pie versus Good Humor; the motorized truck vs. the foot peddled bicycle wagon; Joe versus the Good Humor Man.

My immediate reaction was that of confusion.

"Wasn't all ice cream the same?" I thought naively. I hadn't eaten enough ice cream to know the difference. I didn't know what it meant to make a comparison. All I saw was a rivalry, a battle for the ice cream business on my block.

I would think that Joe would have the advantage, being the first ice cream man on my block. He had a large following, made more visits to our block everyday. He knew his customers. He was trustworthy, friendly and dependable. Joe was also a great salesman, a gentleman always with a smile, and a friendly demeanor who gave away lucky sticks. Even my mother approved of likeable Joe and said that I should buy from Joe and no one else.

But eventually the other children and their parents began to embrace the Good Humor Man and his ice cream. Soon enough, the bicycle wagon had been replaced with an ice cream truck similar to Joe's.

One day, Joe and the Good Humor man came to our block at the same time. As usual, Joe parked his truck at my house. The Good Humor man parked on the other side of the street. It was a warm sunny day and the children and their parents came out in abundance.

They all lined up at the Good Humor Man's truck. There was no one at Joe's truck, except for me. I looked into Joe's eyes and asked for an Eskimo Pie Pop. I could tell he was sad. This was the beginning of his end. This was his livelihood, his world crumbling right before him. He was defeated. He felt betrayed by the children and their parents on the block, but said nothing to me. I felt bad looking at him, as he stared sadly at me in disbelief..

I then made a silent promise to myself. As long as Joe sold ice cream on my block I would always buy from him, and him alone. I felt for Joe, and felt disdain for those who had abandoned him.

A year passed and there was no Joe, and then another. I was now in elementary school with peers of my own age, some of whom had become my friends. Then, on one early spring day, I heard the ice cream bells. Surprisingly, a white truck pulled up and stopped at my house. Out stepped a man clad in white regalia. I looked closer.

Could it be? Would it be?

Oh my G-d, it was Joe coming out of a Good Humor truck. He was a little heavier, baldish, with grey at his temples and in his moustache. He still had the same change maker attached to his belt. It was Joe, reincarnated as the Good Humor Man. I ran towards him and we hugged.

I asked, "How are you? I haven't seen you in more than two years!"

He answered, "I've had some heart problems, but I'm ok now.

I continued, "Are you actually a Good Humor Man now?"

"Yes," he said. "I couldn't beat them. They offered to train me, so I joined them."

"Do you like your new job?"

"It's ok," he said.

I could see that he was not the same man I had known. He still had that upbeat manner although his life experiences had beaten him down.

This was the story of Joe, a simple, hard working man who in my little mind played a memorable role in my young life. For me, Joe was more than an ice cream man. He was my friend when I had none.

The Chicken Man

There was only one window in our house that my mother ever opened. That event took place for the first time that I remembered on the first warm spring day when I was but four years old. Then, the bottom window was opened but three or four inches from the sill, barely enough for me to stand on my toes to look out, in order to cleanse away the stagnant winter stench of our home.

Almost all at once, the revelation for me was the sounds of the street that pierced their way through our house as if they were friendly intruders ushered in from the outside world. As the sun rose to begin the day, the silence was broken by the clanking sound of homogenized glass milk rbottles, which were laid to rest at our doorstop, as if sent by a genie at our sideway entrance door opposite our kitchen.

Then, a yell sounding more like a shriek of a rooster at dawn by a transit peddler crying out "Gevel Water," a water softener which he solicited from our common alleyway adjacent to our house and or next door neighbor.

The day progressed onward as various fruit and fish peddlers made their appearance on our block in their ancient
horse drawn wagons to sell their fresh wares in their own distinctive way. The curiosity for me was whether the animals
would leave their deposit of residue as evidence of their journey on our block.

The insurance man appeared weekly in his starched white
shirt and bow tie, along with his little black receipt book. He
would rap on the door in a forceful way, but was gentle and
congenial in his conversation with my mother as she, in an
arranged situation, quickly gave him a dollar bill each week in
return for a paper receipt. In a flash, like a jack rabbit, he was
gone.

Next, almost magically as if from the heavens on a monthly
basis, I heard the sweet sounds of a fiddler in our alleyway. My
mother quickly took advantage of the moment to come to the
window, draw it open as widely as possible to its maximum
height in order to hear the brilliant lyrical musical notes which
now completely permeated our house, in addition to being
engulfed in the concert hall of our back alley.

I walked to the window and noticed a little man dressed in
black and white with a black hat and a long white beard, and a
handkerchief tucked between his chin and shoulder, fiddling
away, tapping his foot to the ground while playing an upbeat
Yiddish tune. My mother quickly wrapped some coins in a
paper napkin and tied it together with a rubber band and
threw it out the window. He thanked her kindly and continued
playing and then asked her in Yiddish, not missing a note, what
request she wanted to hear.

Her answer was, "*Tum-Balalayke,*" an old Yiddish folk song. He obliged and then was gone in a moment.

Now, beyond the equinox, as spring days became longer and I was allowed to stay up later each day before going to sleep, especially during Sunday evenings when my father, freed momentarily from his six and one-half day work week, was home.

On one such evening after dinner I remember hearing a faint tapping on our kitchen entrance door. Tap, tap, tap, barely above a whisper was the sound I heard, always in a cadence of threes. My mother opened the door, and in walked a man I had never seen before.

I was entranced by his look and demeanor. He nodded to me as if he knew me. I was surprised and wondered to myself who he could be. My mother introduced us. His name was Henry, a friend of my fathers.

Being a precocious child, I asked my mother why he was my father's friend. She said they were childhood friends, a *landsman,* who came from the same town as my father. I became fixated with Henry's features because they seemed so unusual to me. His face had bird-like features, a distinctive long, pointed nose, like a beak. He had high hollowed out cheek bones, deeply recessed eyes, and an angular head adorned with brown hair. He was clean shaven and smelled of cologne.

He was of medium height but he looked taller than he was as a result of the brown hat that he wore and his finely tailored suit with padded shoulders. He was dressed immaculately in what was probably the only suit that he owned, which he only wore on the weekends and holidays.

I found out from my dad, a tailor by trade, that the suit was a product of my father outfitting him from the Orchard Street market stores on the lower East Side. To complete the package, Henry wore a fine beige shirt to go with a brown checkered tie, gold tie clasp, and highly polished brown shoes. From his appearance, he looked like a fashion plate from a men's clothing magazine. I stared at his looks and examined his attire. I watched Henry closely as I quietly whispered to my mother, "Why is he here?"

My mother answered, "For business."

"What business?" I asked

She replied, "Business, just business," as if to silence me.

My curiosity was further peaked with anticipation. What could this business be about, I wondered. The conversations during these Sunday evening meetings were all in Yiddish. Then my mother cried out, "Sam! Henry is here."

My father came into the room, exchanged greetings and, as if programmed, sat down at the breakfront. Henry then said, "Write me out a *tshekl*," pronounced "checkal." My father then opened one of the drawers, took out a large blue bank registry and asked Henry, "How much?"

Henry replied, "For 35."

My father answered in some surprise, "Last week it was 25."

Henry said, almost sheepishly, "It's holiday time."

Dad then wrote out the check and delicately ripped it out of the register and handed it to Henry who snatched it graciously and thanked him in a beholden way. I was fascinated and wide-eyed by the exchange. After some small talk between them, Henry left as quietly as a mouse, in the same manner that he arrived.

I asked my mother, "Why did Daddy give him a *tshekl* and what did it mean?"

She said, "Ask your father," in a less than friendly tone.

I literally took the advantage of that invitation and cornered my father, first asking him about the term *landsman*, and then *tshekl*.

He said that in the old country he and Henry were young children who grew up in the same *shtetl*, or village, and ultimately came to America. He went on to say that Henry was from a very poor family and had no real trade in order to make a living. My Dad said he felt obligated to help him out in America, that a *landsman* is more than just a friend, but that a true *landsman* went out of his way to try to help their own kind.

He said, "That is what true friends are for, that is why I gave him a *tshekl*, money for him to open up his business on Monday mornings."

"What is his business?" I asked.

Daddy replied, "Henry is the neighborhood Chicken Man."

My mother, feeding my curiosity, asked me if I would like going food shopping with her.

It was a Thursday morning. She took her folded up little food wagon with her to the store. We visited the grocery store, the drugstore, and then, the surprise of surprises, Henry's chicken store, only three blocks away from where we lived. The cart had just enough room for a fresh chicken which would be served to begin the Sabbath on Friday evening.

As we walked through the front door I was amazed as I saw this woman, called Gussie, her hair in a net, wearing a blood stained apron and men's shoes, sitting on an old wooden chair, holding a dead chicken in her hands between her spread legs. She was pulling the feathers out of its body rapidly, like a magician shuffling cards. In less than a minute, the bird was naked as she then started on another and just as quickly repeated the process while gabbing away in English and Yiddish, a mile a minute to the female customers. Besides Henry, I was the only male in the store.

The store was completely inhabited by many female Jewish shoppers treading on a floor covered completely in chicken feathers, a two-inch thick layer, not to mention the chicken dust which rained down on the customers.

Gussie was Henry's wife, a short, cherubic, bow-legged woman who was born in America with a nice smile who was happy to have married Henry so late in life to avoid becoming an old maid. She bore Henry two lovely daughters and became more than a devoted wife as she worked in the store as the "chicken flicker."

The store, sandwiched between two other stores, was quite narrow in size and had no windows to provide proper ventilation. Henry always left the front and back doors open to feebly attack the vile stench of dead chickens.

On that Thursday, it seemed as if every Jewish woman in the neighborhood would frequent Henry's store. For that day, Henry was important. He was addressed and recognized as if on a podium like a king.

To my eyes, Henry had gone through a shocking transformation from a dapper Dan, an immaculately dressed gentleman from our first meeting to a man in a matching blood splattered apron similar to Gussie's, adorned with snow white feather dust sprinkled in his cap worn brown hair. That was his distinguished crown as he indulged in gossip conversation and price bargaining with a mixed age assortment of women trying to get the freshest, biggest chicken they could find at the lowest price possible.

Henry took center stage as the ladies in waiting anxiously bombarded him with gruff comments such as "this chicken is too thin, it's not fresh enough, its too small, looks too yellow, its sickly looking, and will it give good soup." Henry replied to this question with, "I didn't ask the chicken." The discussion became more heated and the women became more angry saying that "the chicken isn't clean enough and has too many short leftover feathers." They were always critiquing Gussie's work.

Like a lawyer, Henry defended his wife saying that she used a small flame to sear off the short hairs. He said to the women, respectfully calling them by their last names, Mrs. Schwartz, Mrs. Rosenberg, Mrs. Klein, that his poulets were all first quality chickens which demanded a good price. Being honorable, he said, "I would never sell anybody a bad chicken."

By this time I was getting nauseous, about ready to puke, as a result of the odorous chicken stench which engulfed the narrow room. My mother said, "Stay by the front door and take some breaths of outside air," as she completed her business with Henry. We then left the store to come home with the chicken on top of my mother's cart and I now had all I wanted to know about the chicken business from watching and listening to Henry and Gussie in the chicken store.

The next time I saw Henry was the following Sunday evening. This time the discussion between him and my father was about plots, family plots. As children in the old world, being of peasant stock, they were always concerned with survival and death. My father, along with his *landsman* founded his old village's society in America. He was its first elected secretary-treasurer. His responsibility was to provide cemetery plots for all the members of the society. The cemetery was in Long Island. This insured a place for them and their family when they died.

The discussion was about eternal peace, the size, location, the direction the plot faced, how far from the road it was, how many plots were needed and most importantly, the price of each of the plots. Henry listened intently, but could not be sold by my father of its importance. Henry said over and over again, feeling almost ashamed and embarrassed, "I am a poor man who lives in a small, low rent apartment with two little daughters and a wife, and as much as I would like, I can't afford to buy a family plot."

My father, understanding his situation and using his power of office said he would see what could be done by the society to help Henry. He then said, "See you in *shul* next week for the Jewish holidays." Henry left, taken somewhat aback by what had just transpired during the discussion.

The *shul* was nothing like my father's old temple in his *shtetl*, his village, but was a typical small *shul* in America. Instead, it was my mother's shul, a converted house, reconstituted from her old town in the old country, with the aged rabbi included. Her father and brothers were *Koyhanim*, the selected few high priests of the ancient historical order who were afforded special honors and privileges in the temple. She, being the daughter of a *Koyhanim,* a *Bas Koyhanim,* would sit in the reserved, separated sections of the temple in the first row of women, behind the last row of men. Those undistinguished last rows were filled with the bottom rung of the class order known as the *Yisroels.* This row was occupied by my father, Henry and myself on two counts.

First, my father's last name beginning with a "W" for Winter, and Henry's last name beginning with a "U" placed us there. Secondly, they were both *Yisroel,* primarily followers, ordinary people, with little or no privileges. We all could be seen by my mother if she looked forward and peeked through the thinly veiled curtains. However, we could not see her, or the other women of the gallery unless we conspicuously turned completely around, which was forbidden.

The services went on forever. Being young, having a short attention span, and being bored, I was excused for a while. Later, my father came to get me from one of the anterooms. There was a pause in the prayers and the officers of the *shul* began the fundraisers to get donations from the congregation for various charities.

Everyone was now seated. After a spokesman for the ailing Rabbi gave the sermon, the highest donations came from the center of the *shul* near the *bema,* or high altar, where the *Koyhanim* were seated. The *shamus,* or caretaker of the *shul,* and a *Koyhanim* himself would preside and state the *Koyhanim's* name and the amount of the contribution. "Mr. Schwartz, $100. Mr. Greenberg, $100. Mr. Tenner, $100." This was followed by the second rank in the class structure, the *Levites*. "Mr. Klein, $50. Mr. Gold, $50," and so on. Finally they recognized the *Yisroels*, the bottom rank. "Mr. Brodsky, two *chai* ($36). Mr. Seltzer, one *chai*, $18. Mr. Farber, $15." My father raised his hand. "Mr. Winter, one *chai, $18*," said the *shamus*.

Henry, who wanted to make a donation, looked quickly to my father for advice. My father said, "It's good to give charity to others. Give what you can."

The *shamus* said, "Are there any more donations?"

Henry, feeling the pressure, slowly raised his hand and said sheepishly, "$5.00."

The *shamus* responded by saying, in Yiddish, "*On a nomen*, without a name, $5.00."

The hush and undertone of the noise in the temple ceased. The entire congregation from every direction turned and looked at Henry at that precise moment, as if on cue, because Henry was literally the last man standing. Dead silence followed as Henry sat down. I could see the tears flowing down his face. It was as if he had been speared, but still alive. He had given money, which proportionally, as a poor man, he really didn't have. He did this because my father said it was alright to give something, anything. He trusted my father because he was his mentor, benefactor and friend in America. His *landsman*, he figured, could never intentionally hurt him.

Henry was more than embarrassed or demeaned. He was emasculated, was naked for all to see, to the point of losing his birthright. He was beyond the normal indignity of the *Yisroels*. He was now known as a nameless person to all of the congregants. Henry's pain became my father's pain because he felt responsible and guilty for the dastardly responses afforded to Henry. My father was mad, angry at the congregation, and empathetic towards Henry.

Almost as quickly as Henry had been shot down, the services resumed, as if nothing had taken place. Henry and my father, both seething internally and tearful on the outside continued praying until the services were concluded.

We lived about a mile from the *shul*. Henry lived two blocks from where we lived. It was the longest and yet shortest walk home one could have. Both men's faces were long with despair because Henry's character had been defamed and assassinated. Henry had only come to this temple in the first place on my father's say so. On the other hand, my father felt that he had to please my mother and her family. The pace of the walk home and the time was quickened by their anger. Many remarks were passed between my father and Henry.

Henry at times almost hyperventilated saying, "I gave something. True, it was a small amount but it was something. How could they do this to a person, a human being? What gives them the right to say what they said?" He was crying as he spoke. "To act that way in a house of prayer on a holy day is a sin. Where is there compassion as people to people, especially to a poor man like myself?"

My father used the word *chutzpah* to describe what happened. Being overwrought, my father stuttered and couldn't control himself. He was filled with emotion when he said, "Rather than acknowledging you for your generosity in giving to the poor, while being poor yourself, they made you feel poorer than poor by not thanking you in a proper way. Instead, they insulted you for your charitable contribution by ignoring you, by not even mentioning your name, but still taking your money. That is *chutzpah*, plain and simple. They should be ashamed at how disgusting they were to you."

That was the last time Henry was to attend services at that *shul*. From that day on he attended a house of prayer that was friendly to him, two blocks away from where he lived. Henry told my father how considerate the congregants of this new temple were towards him, valiantly trying to get my father to join as well. My father, although he may have hated to do so, continued to go to my mother's *shul* and sit in the last row.

Henry worked hard as the chicken man and together with his wife, Gussie, somehow managed to provide a college education for both of his girls. Although scarred and getting little respect from others in life, Henry persevered. As the years went by, as if blessed by G-d himself, Henry and his wife lived a long life in good health. Once my father died, and then my mother, I would often visit them to pay my respects at their gravesite. I would always walk through the sacred grounds of the cemetery looking at various tombstones in the family plots of my father's *shtetl* organization.

On one of my visits I walked by and saw the new gravesites of Henry and Gussie Ulberg. They were united together in death as they had been linked together in life, not in a chicken store, but this time side by side on a double monument.

No one could tell that Henry had been disrespected as a poor chicken man, or that he was abused in a *shul* or that he was dependent on others for making his livelihood.

There he lay in peace, in a cemetery with countless others, and only immediate family and friends knowing the true history of those resting souls. For Henry, death was a great equalizer, finally being put to rest on par with others on the same playing field shared by all irrespective of their station in life. As a preschool child witnessing Henry's travails, being touched as a little person, and never forgetting Henry's hardships, Henry, for me, had been vindicated and redeemed forever.

Maybe Henry took for granted what he did in life as being unimportant. Maybe he didn't realize that one of the greatest contributions one could make in life itself is to provide sustenance to others. Not only did he accomplish this task from his work, but he also cultivated the tradition of his people and his culture to flourish ahead in this world of ours.

The Fireman

I lived at 2118 76th Street in Brooklyn, New York City. My family lived in the only unattached two story building on the block. We lived in the downstairs apartment. All the other houses on the block were long and narrow attached homes with the windows of those homes facing each other in the side alleyways. The front entrances of those houses had only one room that actually faced the street. That room in our house was called the sun parlor. Not only could you see the street and its traffic, but you could see across the street and look directly into the sun parlors of the houses on the other side of the street if their shades were open at the same time as yours.

Because my mother was a neat freak, all our windows were dressed with Venetian blinds and curtains. The windows were never opened to prevent noise and dust from entering our home. The coldest room in the house had a large front entrance door and large windows enveloping the room. There was one small, inadequate radiator in the room. The mail was delivered through the front door which had a letter slot cut out for this specific purpose.

Sometimes I would sneak through the narrow rooms of our house and go into the sun parlor, lift up the blinds maybe three inches from the bottom sill and look out into the street to get a good look at the weather and the outside happenings. This was exciting for me because it was like tasting the forbidden fruit. I felt like an explorer.

One day as I looked across the street from my house perch I noticed two real figures in a fixed profile position looking at each other in the house directly opposite from my house. They looked transfixed without any movement whatsoever. This was not a mosaic or the American Gothic or even a portrait, but real figures. They gave the appearance of being framed by the window itself from that distance,

My eyes strained as I tried to figure out what was going on. To me, it looked like two people, one of which was wearing a black hat, jacket, white shirt and dark tie, with the other in a jacket and baseball hat.

What were they doing together during the day for hours on end? Who were they? Why were they doing what they were doing? The less I knew, the more I wanted to know. The unknown fascinated me to find out even more. This spell was broken when my mother called me to eat lunch or dinner.

After my meal I would softly walk back into the sun parlor and peek again. Most of the time, they were still there, in the exact same positions, as if still posing for a picture. This continued day after day. Finally I couldn't resist any longer and asked my mother, "Who are they? What are they doing? Why are they doing it?"

She responded, "Again with the questions. It's not your business. You ask too many questions. Mind your own business." This abruptly ended my inquiry—at least for that moment.

One day I found a red spauldine ball under a car in the street at our curb. I asked my mother if I could keep it to play with. She said it was ok.

My father had a stoop built on the front of our house. It had rounded steps from the street level to meet the first floor level of the house. It was there that I played stoop ball by myself. Once in a while there would be an errant throw and the ball would cross the street. As luck would have it at that precise time the ball rolled across the street. The man who I was looking at in the window across the street returned the ball and walked towards me holding the ball in his hand and said, "Is this your ball son?"

I was speechless, excited and somewhat frightened. I nodded, saying, "Yes." He handed me the ball and I said, "Thank you." Then I asked, "Do you live here?"

He answered, "Right there," as he pointed to the next building to the right of where I lived, "in the downstairs apartment."

"Why are you dressed like that?" I asked.

"Oh, that's my uniform," he answered.

I could now really see his outfit close up, so much more clearly. Everything seemed matched perfectly: the black and white colors of his suit, shirt, tie and shoes He was a handsome looking gentleman with a friendly face, nice smile, well defined adult features and looked tall, strong and powerful. Although his voice was deep his way was tender, soft spoken and caring.

"What's a uniform?" I asked.

He said, "I'm a fireman. That's what I wear when I go to work."

"What does a fireman do?" I continued to ask.

He explained, "As a fireman I try to help people when they have a fire problem, usually in their houses."

"Wow," I said, "Isn't that dangerous?"

"It can be, once in a while. But we were trained how to fight fires of all types," he replied. I was impressed. He was my neighbor, had gotten my ball and was a fireman as well. He asked, "What's your name son?"

I softly answered, "Sid."

He said, "My name is David." He put forward his right hand to shake mine. His hand was large and warm as I placed my little cold hand in his. I felt a sense of great comfort in that act, as if we were now friends.

I next took advantage of the situation and surprised myself by asking what he was doing everyday across the street in the house opposite mine. He answered, "I'm there with Jerry."

"What are you doing with Jerry?"

"Checkers at first, but now chess," he said.

"What's that?" I asked.

"Games," he replied.

"Can I watch sometime?" I asked.

David said, "It will be ok if your mother gives you permission to cross the street by yourself. If that was ok with her, when we are playing, then all you have to do is ring the bell and Jerry would let you in."

I was so pleased. I had met David, and if I could convince my mother, I could also meet Jerry. After all, didn't my mother now allow me to go into the street to buy ice cream from Joe, the ice cream man? Now maybe she would let me go across the street to Jerry's house. David then said that he had to go home. He said, "Goodbye," and then he left.

Once my mother gave me permission to go across the street I felt empowered to ring the bell where Jerry lived. My anticipation overruled my anxiety and nervousness as I rang the bell. David opened the door and said as he pointed to Jerry, "Sid, this is Jerry." I looked at Jerry and was startled by his appearance and manner. He remained seated at the bridge table and did not say a word. He looked at me in a most curious fashion as David grabbed a folding chair and put it in between himself and Jerry for me to watch the game.

I looked into Jerry's large, brown, recessed eyes and noticed that he appeared somewhat awkward and protective, almost as if he were a territorial animal. I quickly realized that Jerry was unlike any other person I had come into contact with in my young life. I was simply stunned, if not shocked, and said absolutely nothing as I recorded forever my first impressions of that memorable day.

They were intently playing chess. This was a game of the mind. Both players took their time in making their moves. David explained, as they played, the purpose of the game, how the pieces moved, and what they were capable of doing. No matter how interesting and fascinating the game was, it could never compare with the lasting impression that Jerry made upon me.

Jerry was unique. He could not speak as we normally speak. He could only make sounds. He could not hold his head erect. He braced it with his hands. He sat on a pillowed chair leaning to one side. He pretty much had little or no control of the motions of his body. He drooled from the mouth. He wore a light brown jacket over a woolen shirt and a baseball hat. He had long, thin, bony fingers which he awkwardly used to move the chess pieces. He was thin-framed in body, his face hollowed out at his high, protruding cheek bones.

The following questions ran through my mind: Is he sick? Why does he look and act the way he does? Is this a temporary thing or is he like this all the time? How old is he? How can he play this game? Why is David really there? Should I even be here? I felt very uncomfortable sitting there, but I was too frightened and shocked to say anything. I felt so helpless in this situation that I wanted to go home. But how could I after I had just invited myself to Jerry's house not five minutes before? I had great expectations of meeting a new friend and having something to do with my time. I realized I was stuck and had to see this experience through to its conclusion. I was intimidated by the sight of Jerry, but calmed by David being there. Thus I became a captive in this strange and different environment.

Once I got over the shock of what I witnessed from closely observing Jerry's characteristics I began to focus on the game itself. What struck me almost immediately was David and Jerry's competitive nature as opponents in the game. David played silently whereas Jerry made startling sounds and gestures showing happiness and excitement when he made an excellent move. At first I rooted for David because of his coolness under pressure. Then I slowly shifted and rooted for Jerry because of his exuberance and charged emotion. They both, to my initial surprise, understood and respected each others feelings and capabilities as they played. In the end, I felt like an impartial referee looking at the beauty of real combatants in a match of brainpower, intellect and wits. Time flew by and the game concluded quickly. Another game was played and concluded. Then David and I began to leave after Jerry shook David's hand and mine. David and I walked to my house across the street. It was at that moment that I asked David about Jerry's condition.

David simply said, "Jerry is a boy like you, actually a young man, who, unfortunately, has a severe and permanent illness which handicaps him from doing a great many things that you or any other young boy could do."

"Will he ever be able to talk?" I asked.

"Not like you," he answered. "He can only make grunts and simple sounds. After a while you will get used to his method of communication and understand what he means."

"Can he walk?" I asked.

"Not very well. His spine is damaged and he needs metal braces to keep his body straight. It is painful and difficult for him to walk."

"Then what can he do?" I asked.

David proudly answered, "He can think. He has a good mind and brain. He remembers things and is quite bright and intelligent. That's why he can play chess very well. He always gives me a good fight in our chess matches."

From David's comments I began to better understand Jerry's problems. I felt sad for Jerry, realizing how tough his life was.

"Does he go to school?" I asked sheepishly.

David replied, "Yes and no."

"I don't understand," I said.

David explained that in good weather a special bus or carrier took him to school, but in bad weather the school came to him. Then a specialhome bound teacher would come to his house. David said, "Anything he learned was so much more difficult for him than it was for any of us. Jerry can write the letters of his first name and slowly read on a simple, elementary level, mostly by recognizing pictures." Jerry apparently had difficulty controlling his muscle groups when holding a book, a chessman, or a piece of paper to write on. David then raised his voice and said clearly, "But don't pity him, accept him."

"What does pity mean?" I asked.

"Don't feel sorry for him or think any less of him because of his condition. Better yet, play with him, be a friend, and treat him as your equal even if he thinks otherwise. That would be the greatest *mitzvah* in our faith that you could give to him."

I felt good now. I knew what *mitzvah* was—doing a good deed, a blessed thing from G-d. I now knew how to act.

David, like my father, was a great teacher, hero and role model. Besides teaching me the rules of checkers and chess, he taught me about moral behavior. I made the realization that no matter how bad I may have felt in my young life at times, there were always people that were worse off than I. Friendship would be the great ingredient in the mix of life. It would always trump pity.

Then David went home. I entered my house with my head held high. I never actually knew what Jerry suffered from, be it cerebral palsy, muscular dystrophy or something else. From that day on I didn't ask; it just didn't matter. What mattered was my being motivated to go to Jerry's house the next day and ring the bell, sit down and play with Jerry. I had quickly come to realize that Jerry was a brave and bright, lucid, friendly and intelligent fellow who was as loveable and as competitive as anyone I was ever to meet in my life. David was the fireman who lit the lamp of learning for me in appreciating life beyond the judgments and first impressions of people and other things. It was part of my young maturation.

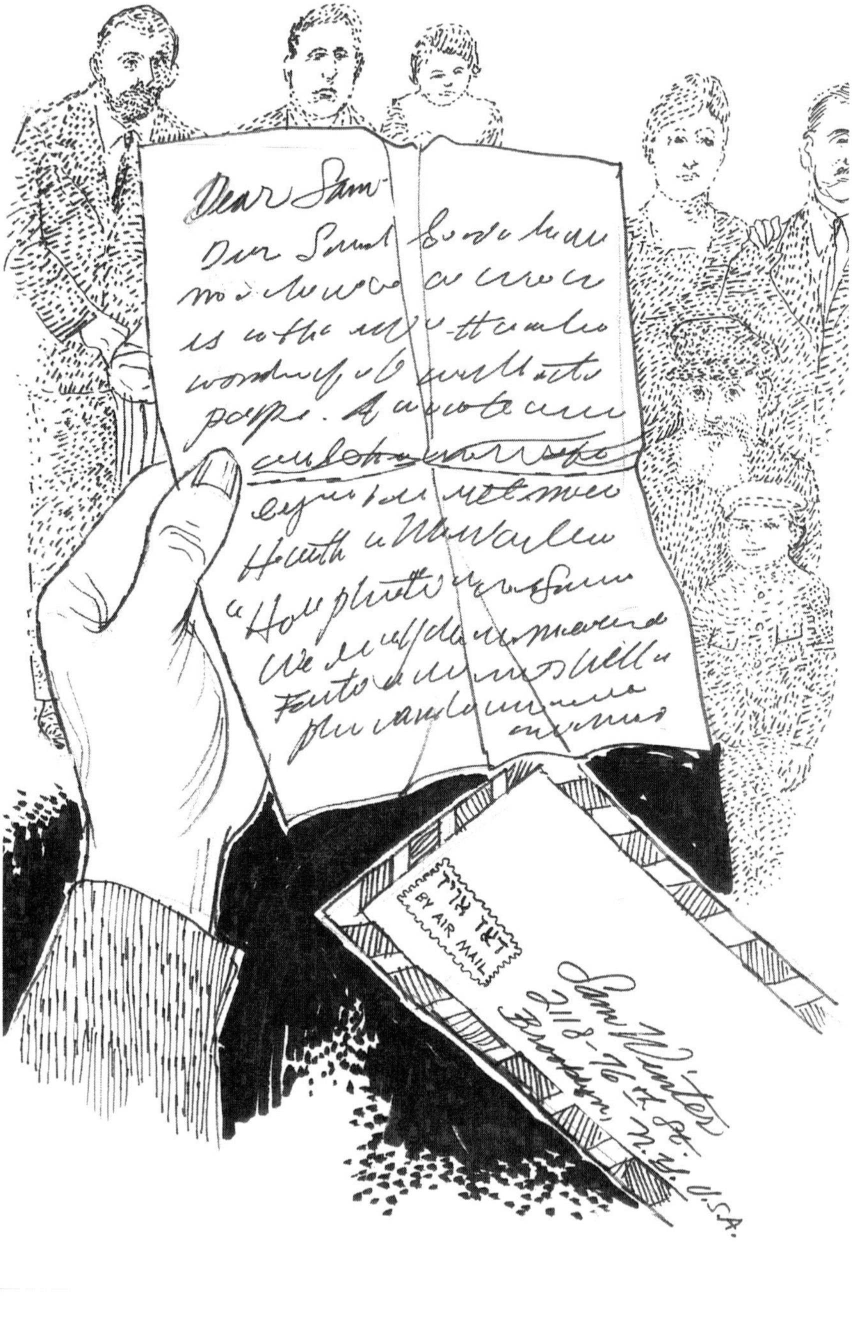
Dear Sam
BY AIR MAIL
U.S.A.

The Letter *(Der Breev)*

The crib that I slept in since birth was a hand-me-down. A brown, cold iron clad gated creature with vertical adjustable rods on the sides for protection. It made me feel captive and isolated. I hated it.

By the time I was four I jimmied the vertical rods in such a way as to free myself from my isolated confinement.

My mother realized that although being quite thin and short of stature, I was a growing boy. To go with that development she delegated responsibilities to me such as getting the mail everyday from the mail slot located near the bottom of our front door in the sun parlor. Like clockwork everyday at about the same time the mailman would make his rounds. I looked forward to this job because I could walk through the house and go to the sun parlor and look outside into the street.

On this day there was something unusual in the mail delivery. Besides the normal items there was a lightweight, thin, blue, tissue-like letter. I had never seen a letter like this before.

It had special writing on the outside of the letter. It stood out from all the other mail in the mix. It also had various stamped markings on the envelope. I scooped up all the mail and left it on the kitchen table, always in the same place, as my mother conditioned me to do. She was immaculate and fastidious to the point of obsession. The furniture in our house was never moved. It was always in the same place. When cleaning you could always place the furniture in exactly the same spot from the past embedded carpet impression of the furniture legs. Now that my chore of picking up the mail was completed, I asked my mother, "Why is this letter different? Who is it from?"

She only replied, "It came from the old world by airplane," and said nothing more. I thought nothing of it and moved on in my own way.

That evening my father came home later from work. As was customary, my mother would wait for him and they would eat dinner together. I saw him for a few moments and then I had to go to sleep. I was restless and had difficulty falling asleep. For a while I lay awake, tossing and turning.

After dinner my parents would read the mail. I dozed off in a light sleep, half awake, half sleeping. I suddenly woke up as I heard my mother say aloud in Yiddish, *"Oy vay iz mir, Oy vay iz mir!"*—*Oh how it hurts me!* —over and over again. Beneath her almost screaming sounds I heard my father bitterly sobbing in a lower register. On and on went the lament, seemingly never-ending.

The year was 1939. I was four years old, and this was the earliest recollection of anything I remembered as a youth. It was never to be forgotten. It became, for me, the darkest of nights.

I quickly escaped from my enclosure and walked into the kitchenette. My parents were hysterical. My mother, looking up at the ceiling, with her hands lifted to the sky, was saying in Yiddish, "*Oy G-t in himl, Oy G-t in himl!*"—Oh G-d in heaven!—repeating it over and over again, each time with more emphasis. My father's eyes were bright red as he continued to cry, saying nothing.

I stood there with my mouth open, looking at both of them as if they were in a different world. They didn't even notice me standing there staring at their horrific pain. I was shocked by their behavior at first, and didn't know what they were crying about. In quiet sympathy tears began to flow down my cheeks. My father then looked at me and said, "this is the last *breev* (letter) from my family."

The reality was that my mother knew, my father knew, and now I knew at the young age of four that there was virtually no hope that this situation would be ever be resolved or change for the better. My mother asked, "What can we do?"

At first my father did not want to answer at all. Then he said, "We'll see." When asked again what could be done, he held his head down in his hands crying and said, "*gournish,*" nothing.

My paternal uncle—my father's older brother who lived in the upstairs apartment of our house—had rescued my father from religious persecution by sending him a ticket to come to America. My maternal grandfather worked for five years in America in order to save money and rescue my grandmother, my mother and her two brothers so they too could come to America. My father quickly knew in his heart of hearts that there was no way to rescue his parents, two sisters, their husbands and their two young children. He knew from past history and the contents of the *breev* that they all would perish. It was the family's final goodbye.

Another letter never came, although I looked for one every time I got the mail from the sun parlor. There was nothing, always nothing, to be found.

That solemn evening defined all of our lives. We would never be the same people as before. My mother was angry—which she openly displayed by cursing and damning our enemies when war broke out in Europe the same year. My father's philosophy of life was formed from that dastardly moment onwards. To his great credit, for the rest of his life, he first became an air raid warden on our block during the war. Afterwards, he was instrumental as a Zionist by planting trees in Israel, buying bonds and contributing money to a fledgling state. He embarked upon a personal crusade to rescue lost family refugees all over the world. When that avenue dried up he would help many refugees to find a place in America or Israel. He received many plaques and awards, and was honored by the societies he worked for, for his unselfish efforts.

It was as if his entire emotional and psychological makeup had changed from great sorrow, helplessness, sadness and feeling victimized to being a proactive, sensitive, dedicated and purposeful person. He literally recovered from the initial tale of woe of the *breev* and its unfortunate circumstances to be resigned in becoming a benevolent soul.

As for me, that experience subconsciously may have been one of the great turning points in my life. The letter became an indelible tattoo in my mind. Although *breev* may sound similar to the word "brief" in English, the episode was anything but short, as it manifested itself in my dreams as I continued to mature.

Little did I know at four that I would someday revisit that evening as a history teacher, preordained to teach about the Holocaust. The *breev* was my own personal *Kristallnacht* as it shattered and disturbed the solitude and peace in my young life and awakened an awareness in myself which I carry with me to this very day.

The Chair

The year was 2007, the month was September, the day was relatively uneventful and boring until I saw a picture of a chair in the furniture section of the New York Times. This, in itself, was not an unusual occurrence for most people, but for me it triggered a meaningful response to memorable events in my life.

The chair was a short, low to the ground, Danish modern molded hard cardboard stuffed barrel chair upholstered with high quality durable royal blue fabric and walnut wooden legs. It was the first piece of furniture that my wife and I had bought after we got married.

This further evoked the memory of the light brown leather tufted button down chair that my father gave us as a gift when we bought out first home.

As I went to the post office with a large envelope for mailing, I noticed a picture of a Chippendale chair as one of the four cent commemorative stamps needed to send my package.

On a trip to Manhattan, in New York City, walking outside of the Port Authority bus terminal building, I stopped and noticed the bronze statue of Ralph Cramden, the fictional Brooklyn bus driver portrayed and commemorated for the working man by the famous actor Jackie Gleason in the very successful T.V. series known as the "The Honeymooners."

These seemingly unrelated events and occurrences by themselves have no significant relevance to just anything or anybody. However, for myself, they are quite pertinent in remembering a profound and defining conversation that I had with my father as a preschool child some 67 years ago. I remember it all as if it were yesterday…

One day before I ever went to kindergarten in our neighborhood public school, I felt very sad. As a lonely little boy I had no male or female friends who were my age that lived on our block. My sister Helen was five years older than I and was already attending elementary school full time. My two maternal uncles and their wives never had any children of their own. My mother was quite busy being a meticulous, if not obsessive, housewife taking care of our two bedroom downstairs apartment in the Bensonhurst section of Brooklyn in New York City. I was a sickly, thin, short kid with no one to play with who internally yearned for someone, anyone to be part of my life.

It was then, after my parents were through having dinner, that I walked over to my father and suddenly, for no apparent reason to them, began to cry. I was despondent and said nothing to my parents. Although I wanted to talk, nothing came out of my mouth but the sad sounds of despair as the tears flowed continuously down my cheeks. I just couldn't stop crying no matter how hard I tried to control myself. Instead, my crying only got worse, bordering on hysteria.

My father then put his soft gentle hand on my shoulder and quietly in his own way asked me what was wrong. His hand on my shoulder felt like magical medicine that immediately began to take effect to make me feel better. He said, "Tell me, what's the matter?"

I answered, "I'm crying because I'm sad and lonely and have no friends." I continued to cry some more and eventually stopped.

He then paused for a moment, looked into my eyes and said, with tears running down his face, "I will be your friend." I cried once more when I noticed that he was crying too.

For the first time in my life I realized that without saying much at all, my father really understood what I was saying and feeling. He was truly emotionally empathetic to my needs as a young child.

I felt good, really good, knowing that he wanted to be my friend. However, I thought to myself, could this really work? He was a grown man. I was a little preschool kid. What did we have in common besides his being my Dadee and I being his little son? "How could you be my friend?" I asked, and then went on to say, "Dadee you come home late from work mostly all the time, so how can we play together?"

He replied, "I will always find the time to listen to you like I am doing right now."

"What else can you do besides listen?" I asked in a somewhat demanding way.

He said, in a sincere manner, "I will tell you stories from my life when I was a little boy living in the old country."

I asked, "What does that mean?"

He said, "I will tell you where I lived, how I lived and what I did when I was your age. I know what it is like to be lonely and have no friends. I didn't have time to play because I had chores to do. Everyone in our house worked. We had no time for games or friends. We had to survive…"

I, in my own way, tried to digest what he had said and then blurted out, "What about me? What could I do?" I wanted to take part in the dialogue my father was trying to establish between us.

He expounded upon what he had said. "You could carefully listen and ask me questions about my life experiences and I will try to best answer you."

I couldn't believe what I had just heard. I was overwhelmed and comforted at the same time. I could actually ask all kinds of questions, anything I wanted to ask about his past life. I somehow gained a little confidence and impulsively asked, "Could I begin to ask you questions right now?"

My father seized the moment and said, "Ok."

Playing along and taking an earlier cue from my Dad I asked, "How did you live in the old country?"

My father, the most unlikely storyteller due to a lifelong speech impediment of stuttering and stammering, slowly, deliberately and self-consciously measured his response. His poise and statements were impeccable as he clearly related the story of how he lived with his family in the old country. He described the large hole in the ground that was dug in the middle of the large all-purpose room of his house.

"Why did you have a hole in the ground of your house?" I asked. He said that it was a place where all the perishable items were stored, such as milk, butter and cheese. "Why there?" I asked. He said that the hole was like a refrigerator of today and was very effective in keeping the food fresh and cold so that it would not turn or spoil. "Couldn't you fall into the hole?" I asked. He said the hole was covered with a large cloth and removable wood floor boards which were placed on top of the hole. I said, "You mean you didn't have a refrigerator like we have in our kitchen?"

"That's right. That was mostly unheard of in the old country. Things like that were only for rich people, not for poor people like us or our kind…"

"What kind?" I asked.

"Peasants. Jewish peasants," he said.

"What's a peasant?" I asked.

He said, "They were poor farm workers who had very little of anything in the world."

Being very excited I could not restrain myself and confessed to my father that I was afraid of our refrigerator. He was puzzled by my statement and asked why. I said, "Mamee doesn't let me open the refrigerator door anymore because one time I didn't close the door properly. I noticed that when I closed the door the light would go off. I thought I had broken the refrigerator door!" I had also noticed the little box near the top of the refrigerator with snow and ice on the sides and asked what it was. He explained that it was the freezer that kept fish, meat and chicken from spoiling, and that it was colder than the refrigerator.

I went on to say that "Mamee cleans the refrigerator all the time and I'm afraid to touch it because I don't want to leave my finger marks on the door handle to make the refrigerator dirty. I do want to know what's inside the refrigerator, but Mamee's rules are that the refrigerator is off limits to me until I grow up."

The refrigerator was the brightest object in our kitchen, as if it had a halo around it or a spotlight shining on it. My mother took great pride in washing, polishing and cleaning the refrigerator all the time. I could see the reflection of myself in the door. It was my mother's kitchen masterpiece. It was part of her domain and reflected her work as a fastidious housewife.

This was her full time job—being the general of the house— seriously responsible for the laundry, shopping, cleaning, and polishing everything in sight such as windows, doors, floors, tables, chairs and every other stick of furniture in the house to the point of excess. There was no dust to be found anywhere. She, being of peasant stock with no material possessions of her own in the old country, took great pride in living in and taking care of a house with valuable possessions proudly provided by my father in the new country.

Being more than fascinated with the hole in the ground story, I asked my Dad to tell me another story about himself in the old country. He continued by saying, "My brother and I slept together on a bed of potatoes placed in rows on the dirt floor of the small house in the corner of the big all purpose room."

"Didn't that hurt your back?" I asked.

He answered, "A mattress of old rags filled with hay was sown together and placed on top of the bed of potatoes."

"Why did you and your brother sleep together?"

He said, "That was the thing to do in a cold house in order to stay warm, especially during the winter months. Our body heat was important for us to survive. We didn't have a thick bedspread like you have when you go to sleep." I told him that I heard funny sounds in my bedspread when I went to sleep at night and in the morning.

"Those are *groschen*, old Russian coins, that your mother gave me to sew into you bedspread to keep away evil spirits."

"Are there evil spirits?" I asked, concerned.

"No," he said, and continued his story.

"We slept together until my brother became a young man and decided to go to Amerika."

I asked, "Why were the potatoes on the dirt floor?"

"The potatoes were what we lived on and relied upon every day of our lives. Not only did they serve as a foundation for our bed, but they were also the foundation and food staple of our diet. We stored the potatoes on the dirt floor because they never spoiled in any kind of weather.

Potato *latkehs* and potato *kuguel* were eaten during the Jewish holidays. During the week, potatoes were also used to make bread and soup which we ate all the time. We also cooked, fried, baked, boiled and mashed them, even making *schnapps,* whiskey, out of the potato peels. They were the staff of our life because we were so poor and had little variety of other foods such as meat and fish which we only ate on special occasions. We mostly lived on chicken and potatoes."

"Why did your older brother and you go to America?" I asked.

My father answered by saying, "As kids, they heard stories that Amerika was the 'land of opportunity,' even that the 'streets were paved with gold.'

"Although that wasn't true, we heard that you could *machen a leben*, make a living, in Amerika. You could get rich, live well, have religious freedom and, most importantly, not be discriminated against because you were Jewish…that you could begin a new life there, provided you were willing to work long and hard."

"Did you both go together to America?" I asked.

"No," he answered. "My older brother went first. I was still young when he left. I was the baby of the family. My parents and my two older sisters all remained in the old country along with their married husbands and children."

"Wouldn't your brother and you miss your mother and father?" I asked.

"Yes, that's true, but we really had no choice in the matter."

"Why not?" I asked.

"Because we did not want to serve as soldiers in the Russian Army. We heard terrible stories about what had happened to those soldiers."

"What kind of stories?" I asked.

He replied, "Most young men wanted to avoid the dreaded draft or be literally grabbed right off the street, sucked up anywhere and put into the ill-equipped army which had few guns or proper clothing for most of their soldiers. Very often these soldiers were never heard from again. For that reason alone many men ran away and left their country, never to return, and went to Amerika—if they were lucky enough to have saved enough money for the one-way ticket."

My father went on to say that his brother told him about the horrid three file army system that the Russians used in fighting.

The first line had guns and a uniform; the second line behind the first had sticks and parts of a uniform; and the third line had nothing at all. The soldiers would move up in their ranks to the first row as their fellow soldiers were killed off at the front of the line.

He then related the story of my maternal grandfather Max Tenner who had been drafted into the Russian Army to fight in the Russo-Jap War of 1904. "Your grandfather said that he was sent by Trans Siberian Railroad car nearly 3000 miles across the frozen wasteland known as Siberia to fight the Japanese in a war that the Russians lost. The weapons froze as did their meager food supply. The bread ration froze so badly that you grandfather and other Russian soldiers had to pee on the bread in order to soften it so they could eat it, or else they would starve to death."

"He, after the war, lucky enough to survive, left his family, wife, your mother, and her two brothers and went to Amerika where he worked for five years to save enough money to send for his family to come to Amerika."

I was quiet as a mouse as I intently listened, my ears taking in every word which had been spoken by my Dad. I was shocked beyond anything that I could possibly imagine in what I had just heard. I now understood why my Uncle Joe, my father's older brother, provided the ticket for my father to come to America. Uncle Joe told my Dad, "Be prepared, learn a trade, leave home and start a new life. I will help you get established in the new country." His brother worked as a tailor, who rented and worked in a cleaning store, fixing and pressing garments.

"Weren't you afraid to go to America by yourself?" I asked.

He answered, "Although I was a young man of 25 years of

age, I looked forward to a new beginning in a new country. I went by ship, the *Lapland* from Antwerp, Belgium in September of 1922, to Ellis Island, New York City, where I registered, was met by my brother and taken to his rented home where he lived. I stayed there for a little while until I got settled. Then I had to make a living again, *machen a leben,* to support myself."

"What does 'making a living' mean?" I asked.

He said, "Everyone has to work in life to survive. Your mother, myself, your sister and even you. Everyone has a job to do. I have to work to make money so that I can put food on the table, live in a house, have clothes, pay for everything, electricity, heat, water and anything else."

"What is my job," I asked.

He said, "Your job is going to school to learn."

"What's Mamee's job?"

"Her job is to take care of the house."

"And your job Dadee? What do you do to make a living?"

"While living in Sochachov, my old country *shtetl*, I learned at a young age to work as an apprentice tailor. Before I go further into what I do, I will tell you a true story, my story of what happened to me so that you can better understand how things work and get done in Amerika."

I couldn't wait for this tale. I was bursting at the seams. A real live true story told by my father, my newfound friend, confiding in me like I was an adult. I would forever come to relish this special moment between us for a lifetime.

This was the story of "The Chair."

My father's tone had changed completely. He began to raise his voice and speak with emotional fire and brimstone.

He began by saying, "Once I got settled, my brother, your Uncle Joe, sent me to a shop that he knew of where I might get a job. I went there, knocked on the door, entered the shop and asked to speak to the boss. I said, 'I was sent here by my brother who told me you give tryouts for a job in your shop as a tailor.'"

My father continued, "I was very nervous, but still feeling confident because I was a trained apprentice in the old country who knew his trade. I was young, energetic and had good eyesight, good hands and was willing to work like my brother in order to have a job, make money, and be just as self sufficient as he was in Amerika.

"The boss came to me and said, 'Sit down at the Singer Sewing Machine. Here is a pattern and material. I want you to make me a garment from this material right now.' And then he left. I worked ever so carefully and when I finished the garment I brought it to the boss, feeling quite confident that I had done a good job. The boss looked at the garment and said, 'This is wonderful. You have made me a beautiful garment. You work very well, but I can't give you a job.'

"I looked at the boss and said, 'Why not?'

"He said, 'Do you see this *chair*? The *chair* that you sit on? This *chair* is supposed to produce five garments in the time you produced one garment. That is the reason why I can't use you.' I pleaded with him and asked him please, *please* give me another chance, let me try again… The boss agreed and gave me additional material to make more garments. Using all the skills I learned as an apprentice, I then proceeded to work like a beaver. When I finished in the time allotted to me I had made seven garments. The boss was quite satisfied and gave me a job.

That's how I got to making a living, *machen a leben*, in Amerika."

My father went on to say that in America men were looked upon as failures if they could not provide for their wife and family. It was a badge of honor to make a living and be a good provider. He was proud of the fact that before he married my mother he had worked hard, saved money and bought our house, having the means to entirely furnish the eight rooms that we lived in for so many years. This included the Frigidaire, the modern crown jewel appliance of our kitchen. These were the fruits of his successfully making a living.

"What's more," he boasted, "In the Great Depression of 1929, of the 30 homes on our block, only 3, ours being one, were not taken by the banks for failing to meet mortgage payments."

***

Later on in my life as a mature person recalling how truly realistic my father's traditional story of the chair was, I saw the relevance of how profound the chair was in concerning every facet of my father's life. The chair became the turning point in his life. It defined his being, philosophy, and soul as a person for the next fifty years as a laborer. It became his own monument as a symbol of his pleasure and pain in earning a living.

He became a workaholic, a conditioned work beast, never missing a day, working six and a half days a week until he retired and took social security at age 65. Even then, he proceeded to work part time until his mid-seventies.

He was so conscientious, dependable, reliable, and stable as a worker that the boss entrusted him with the keys to the business, or *gesheft* in Yiddish, to open the shop. By getting up and out at 4:30am every morning he could catch the early train and always be the first one on the job each and every work day of his life.

During the slack season when there was little or no work he was rarely ever laid off. If that did occur, he worked part time in a variety of dry cleaning stores doing miscellaneous tailoring, which he sometimes continued to do when he resumed his ordinary work schedule after the slack season was over.

The sewing machine became an appendage to his self. He bought an old surplus Singer sewing machine and an old straight back green wooden chair from his boss, whom he worked for in the Bronx, and had it delivered to our house in Brooklyn. The sewing machine was equipped with accessories including needles, spools of thread, buttons, zippers, pins, marking chalk, eyehooks and various fabrics of all kinds so that he could do additional work during what little spare time he had when he was home.

My mother was not thrilled with his obsession and compulsion for yet more work.

The day that I heard the anecdotes of the chair, the Russian Army, the potato saga, and the hole in the ground tales was an especially wonderful and glorious experience for a young preschool child who was all ears at that time. However, the story telling oration by my father was quite an exception to the norm. I hardly ever saw him at all except late at night or sometimes on Sunday afternoons when he was off work.

During that special story telling day my father meant well

enough to understand my personal dilemma, but such conversations were so few and far between that I was able to remember every detail of them, details that were stored in my memory bank to draw upon later in my lifetime.

My father received a great informal education by being fully engaged in the capitalistic work habitat known as the sweat shop. He experienced being part of that specialization and division of labor that classified workers according to their skills. These were the cutters, or *shneiders* in Yiddish, pressers, stitchers, packagers, and distributors, along with the ever present supervisors, foremen and models. They, in one way or another comprised the factory system's labor force. They were all part of the defined scripted work ethic and economic system employed by and utilized by the chief entrepreneurs, the bosses.

Among the working class were people of all cultural and ethnic persuasions, who, like my father, labored endlessly by adapting and conditioning themselves to the sweatshop techniques of the economic system that programmed them to be producers and providers in order to survive in this country.

The rewards were monetary, providing the means necessary for a life of materialistic consumption. These material rewards were achieved through my father's eyes at the price of losing one's self dignity. Although on one level my father liked reaping those rewards, he was ambivalent and resented the capitalist system because of the exploitation of working people like himself in the sweat shops.

On yet another level, the exploitation of the workers in the sweat shop was played out not as an institution of slavery, or indentured servitude, but as an opportunity based on strength of purpose to endure and successfully survive. The realization was to be strong, never to miss a day and always perform at peak efficiency.

To the capitalist, time was money. The boss encouraged competition among the workers by providing piece work to his laborers. They would get paid by the number of completed garments they produced. Bonus incentives were offered to the best workers. Workers were ranked not only according to competency but also by their speed in producing and completing tasks.

My father deplored piece work—it took advantage of green horns, new unskilled immigrants—and was merely a means to an end for the entrepreneur to make more money. He felt man was reduced to secondary status being disrespected and shown a lack of humanity.

It was truly survival of the fittest in their adaptation to that work environment. Extinction was the result of not being able to conform to these job standards.

My mother, being emotionally immersed in what she saw as my father's exploitation by the capitalistic culture, uniquely called it a "murder world." She was in complete agreement with my father about workers being disrespected, exploited, and treated as nothing more than hired hands.

For her, the "murder world" went beyond the workplace as a negative expression damning the character and deeds of people in power who abuse the trust of the public through corruption, greed, and breaking the moral and civil codes of law that are supposed to peacefully govern humans.

For these reasons and many more, my father became active in his labor union, seeking health benefits, better working and safety conditions, pay increases, the elimination of piece work and, most importantly, the abolishment of sweat shops.

He went further beyond union involvement to a higher level of political activism, especially during the 1929 depression, by being a communistic sympathizer, embracing left wing liberal political philosophies. He never wanted to become an entrepreneur or go into business. Instead he became a fervent Zionist. He was exceedingly charitable with his money by endorsing the state of Israel and helping survivors of the Holocaust to find their way to America or Israel.

Although my father was quite serious in his demeanor, he enjoyed life to the fullest by deriving great pleasure when he sang songs along with his brother on a few Sunday afternoons when they only worked half a day. There was never any stuttering then, just the joy of expression and happiness. During that period of leisure time they acted as though they were kings. They bought jumbo frankfurters and drank bumper bottles of bock beer when it was in season from the Kosher deli on 20th Avenue and 75th Street in Brooklyn. Sometimes they felt high enough to bang out rhythms with their feet on the wood floors.

My father had a stocky build, about 5'4" tall with powerfully built strong legs that became quite developed from lots of running and walking in the old country. His hair was thin, straight and reddish blonde in color. His appearance was somewhat Nordic with his exceedingly fair complexion, almost white as snow. He was quite strong, never missed a day of work, and never complained of any physical maladies.

However, one day we got a telephone call from his boss, saying that my father had collapsed in his work chair and that he was being sent home by taxicab. My father told us not to worry, that he had medical coverage from his union that had bought a building fully equipped with medical provisions and doctors to care for its members.

My father and I spent the next two days in the medical center where he was given various diagnostic tests for all parts of his body, commonly referred to as the blue plate special. The results revealed that he had an enlarged heart, an enlarged prostate gland and an advanced form of cancer, leukemia. The doctors expounded upon this by saying he had about five years to live. It was about at that time that he became quite tired every day and decided to take social security, working only part time when possible.

Quickly I saw a change in my Dad's physical and mental attitude. He now had difficulty threading a needle. His eyes would swell up and become red, sometimes tearing from eye strain. His hands began to shake uncontrollably. The veins in his hands and fingers were swollen, being so pronounced and throbbing that they looked as if they would pop out and burst. Sometimes in his pain and sadness he would say, "*Ich bin oysgeshpeeled*," meaning "I'm played out."

This became his own personal tragedy, the tragedy of a tailor. A span of more than fifty years had passed of continuous unbroken tailoring with no gold watch rewards, no hall of fame, only knowing he was an unheralded warrior to his family: a provider, an arbiter, a worker, a *fardeener*, Yiddish for a wage earner, and a person who made a good livelihood. The chair that he sat in for all those years became his accepted throne from where he, like a monarch, controlled his own destiny. It gave him the free will to make his own decisions and choices and the opportunity to live his life in his own way, to save for a rainy day, fearful of a repetition of the depression of 1929 which always seemed to loom over his head.

But what if he had failed that very first time when he had his "tryout" in the sweatshop chair? What would his life have been like from that moment on? Would that experience have forced his hands and mind to go beyond being a tailor with a third grade night school education? How would the lives of our family, myself included, have changed? One can only speculate about those queries and ponder long and hard about what might have happened.

However, there is one thing I do know. My father never questioned his decision not to go beyond that of being a tailor. For him it was nirvana. He had no regrets. He was satisfied with his life. In retrospect, little did he surmise that the chair was both his calling, and his falling.

About five years later he was admitted to Mount Sinai hospital in Manhattan before the Jewish high holy days. He and my mother were under the impression that he would be there for a short while and would be home for the holidays. The doctors never told either of my parents that he might not come home at all due to the serious hemorrhages he was being treated for. In fact, he did not end up dying from leukemia at all, but from heart failure.

His legacy was a few bank book accounts, a portrait of him as a vibrant young man in the prime of his life before he became engaged to my mother, and over thirty bottles of

Sunsweet prune juice which he and my mother had accumulated due to chronic constipation from their starchy potato diet.

I still possess the green wooden chair my father brought home to sit in front of his sewing machine. The chair, no longer used for sewing, remains serviceable in its new function. The chair now holds its place of honor in my garage, where I use it as a stool to retrieve household objects stored on the uppermost shelf. It bears my weight well, as though my father is steadfastly supporting me when the need arises.

What did the story of the chair symbolize for me? What was the significance of the chair? How did it affect my life? These are the questions I asked myself throughout my lifetime.

I reflected back in time and of the many uses of the chair in our history from kings to killers, from childhood highchairs and potty-seats for young tots, to seats of power for presidents, dictators and entrepreneurs, to the less powerful and infirmed.

In ancient times the sedan chair was used to carry a victor or hero aloft in military triumph. In the Jewish faith, at weddings, the bride and groom are carried high up in a chair to celebrate the joy of their marriage. Chairs have been used in modern times in sports, for example chair lifts. Chairs have been used to store money in their stuffing, and used as part of a game in musical chairs. Ben Franklin gave us the rocking chair in colonial times. However, there is no actual beginning to the chair that we know of. The origin of the chair could possibly go back to prehistoric times: a smooth stone with an arched back covered with grass or wrapped in animal skin.

But for me, a chair will never be simply a chair, thanks to my father.

The Dish

The Tenner brothers first made their mark in America as produce peddlers in Brooklyn's Bensonhurst section of New York City. The only evidence attesting to this event actually occurring is one remaining green faded dish embossed in gold lettering. The dish was but one of many dishes that were given at that time, free of charge, to the customers on the eventful day that a new general food market opened its doors to the public. The inscription of the dish read, "Tenner's Fruit Store at Wasserman's Market 2233-65th Street."

The discovery and sight of that dish, found while recently cleaning out my mother's old china cabinet, became the kindling to ignite the nearly forgotten memory of my youth and beyond in writing about some of the ensuing experiences of the immediate members of my family.

It was from this produce store that the brothers Tenner learned the craft of retail business. Difficult as it was for them, they learned enough meager English to be able to communicate with and please their customers.

Using their ingenuity, they had connected an old bathtub to the store's plumbing system where they bathed the various fruits and vegetables to keep them fresh and appealing to their clientele. It was there that they further developed their entrepreneurial skills to go beyond fruits and vegetables to graduate to the more lucrative endeavor of preparing and selling fresh fish. They decided to work in two separate stores to make a better living.

The Jewish holidays were always a time of great preparation in our household. Also, it was then that my mother would be asked to help my two uncles at the fish store on Avenue O in Brooklyn. I, being a preschool child, would have mixed feelings about having to go on this journey.

At first my Uncle Harry worked his own rented fish store as part of a general store on Avenue O where they sold fruits, appetizers, groceries, fish and other items. It was during this time that my Uncle Jack, who worked in his own fish store on 18th Avenue, had an accident that nearly brought his working career in the fish store to a forced conclusion. He put an ice pick through his middle finger on one of his hands, causing severe nerve damage to that hand. He no longer had the dexterity that was necessary to complete whatever function was needed in preparing the fish.

As a curious young kid I would always look at his swollen finger which was about three times as large as the rest of the fingers on his hand. This was the primary reason for his leaving the fish store on 18th Avenue and working side by side with his brother in the Avenue O store. It was at that store that they became known as the Fisher Brothers, or the Fishers.

My Uncle Harry, being young, energetic, exceedingly good and fast with his hands, became quite astute with working with the fish. I was always astonished when observing how he worked in the fish store. I would watch as the women would come into the store.

Sometimes he would refer to them as *yi'denehs*, in Yiddish, older Jewish women who were looking for great bargains. These women were quite picayune and meticulous about how they wanted their fish prepared. Firstly, they would look in the large fish tank where there were big live carp swimming around in circles. They would point to the one that they would want and my Uncle Harry would pull out the fish with a special net and throw the caught fish on a wooden board. Then, using a wooden mallet he would bang the head of the still wailing carp until it was semi-unconscious.

At that precise moment he cut the fish open and filleting it, cutting off the head, tails and fins, and then cutting it in slices, salting it and preparing it for the customer. All this was done in a matter of seconds as the customers intently watched the operation. I would look at what had just happened in amazement because I was seeing a live animal being cut into pieces, in seconds, right before my eyes. From that experience I swore to myself never to eat fish for the rest of my life, but I learned at that early age that my Uncle Harry was someone who awed and fascinated me.

Because it was so busy at that time of the year, my mother would help out in packaging and Kosher salting the fish. This would allow the customers to move quickly in line to complete their holiday shopping.

Because the fish smell was so appalling to me I was looking for any avenue of relief to get out of the fish store. After a while my uncle would sense that I would get nauseated, and ship me off to Ida, the attractive blonde, blue-eyed candy story lady, who had a separate store next to the general food store. She would be kind and give me a big three-glass malted milk in order to "fatten me up" and take away the bad taste of the fish store. Being thin as a rail as a kid I gladly sat on a high stool eating pretzels with my malted milk.

When I got tired and bored of the candy store I had permission to visit Willy the baker. His bakery was about two stores next to the candy store. It was there that I was exposed to the delightful sights and smells of brownies, seven layer cake, napoleons, cream puffs and petit fours. I sampled and ate charlotte ruses and éclairs.

Although it was risky to make the change from fruit to fish, my uncles quickly adapted to this new venue in order to make a better living. They became business people who surrounded themselves with other business friends. They began to think like capitalists and favored the free enterprise system. They, being the opposite of my father, had no union affiliation. My Uncle Harry drove a car, a truck, and was a dashing extrovert gay blade who enjoyed the fast life, whereas his older brother Jack was more conservative, introverted and reserved.

The Tenner brothers were so successful as fishers that eventually after World War II, primarily influenced by Uncle Harry, a shrewd risk taker, they bought a farm house that had been converted into a small hotel in the Catskill mountains. It was there that they became big small time hotel entrepreneurs. And so even today, as I gaze at the dish that came from my uncles' store, it reflects my memories of the Woodbine Hotel.

**

The Woodbine Hotel proved to become for me a defining moment that changed my young life. In its first year of operation by the Tenner brothers, my parents sent me to the hotel on the premise so I would eat, gain weight, and breathe the healthy, clean country air. There, in the midst of the Catskill Mountains, often referred to as the Jewish Alps, I learned how to be an innovator, a risk taker, and to use my own ingenuity to become a small time creative capitalist.

For ten years, from age 12 to 22, I would spend each and every summer working at the Woodbine Hotel, nestled among other similar hotel establishments on Ulster Heights road in the surrounding area of Ellenville, New York.

At first, I began working as a water boy who also set up various card games by laying out card tables and chairs in the outdoor shade under deciduous trees, or in the bright sunlight. I brought ice-cold water from the hotel's artesian spring wells to the obsessively thirsty card players.

In addition, I would buy cases of pinochle and poker playing cards, wholesale, with my own money, for my own fledgling little business. I would provide the new packs of cards for the guests to fully indulge themselves in these leisure time activities before and after every meal served at the hotel. For the guests, gambling became a habitual compulsion. For me, it became a profitable business. For my services rendered they would cut a small amount of money from every large moneyed pot and put it into the empty card box containers. That money would grow and grow throughout the card sessions during the day and would be given to me as a lump sum tip for booking and soliciting the players, as well as providing the tables, chairs, umbrellas and well water.

As if that were not enough, I began to provide ice cold buttermilk from my Uncle's refrigerator and sometimes even ice cream at the conclusion of each card session. Needless to say, Uncle Harry was not pleased with my using his own stock. We worked out an arrangement whereby I would invest and provide my own money to replace his stock provided he left a little corner in the hotel's large walk in refrigerator freezer for my own labeled stock.

Each day I would make more money in total overall tips than the largest winner in the highest stakes poker games. So began my entrepreneurial career at age 12.

In that first year I made more money than the 19-year-old lazy bellhop, who gained 20 pounds spending his days laying on the sofa in the hotel lobby. The next year I made even more money, building upon my first year experiences as the water boy, by becoming a multifaceted gaming concessionaire. I provided sodas and drinks of all kinds, including cigars. As such, I catered specifically to the card players' every needs to go along with my new responsibility of now being the one and only bellhop.

It was only a matter of time, through hustling and a strong work ethic, acquired from observing my father as a youth that I moved up the work ladder from my seat in the lobby as a concessionaire bellhop to the dining room as a bus boy, then as a waiter, and finally as a head waiter in my late teens.

As time progressed I began to learn the ropes of the hotel business, the buying and selling of food stuffs, the preparation of food and the creation of menus in the kitchen and dining room. As a young teen, I became the confidant of my uncle. I became his advisor in hiring staff musicians and booking talent shows. When I got my drivers license at age eighteen I also became a part time chauffer for the hotel. By the time I was nineteen I had, to a great degree, learned the fundamentals of how to be a budding hotelman.

During one season I brought two of my closest neighborhood city friends with me to work as busboys. It was also during that summer season that I met my wife to be while I was working as a waiter and she as a counselor.

While at the hotel, growing up during those summers, I was influenced by older people, usually working college students in the dining room as well as people who earned their living in the food service industry by listening, watching, and learning about life. Those experiences expanded my horizons as an adolescent, teenager and young adult.

***

My Uncle Harry was a dominant personality. He was a tall, handsome, charming, extroverted man who sported a great stylish appearance that craved attention, being in the limelight and loving to make grandiose speeches. He was an outgoing, natural salesman, a huckster who was well liked. He had the gift of gab and he was adored, especially by women.

This included my Aunt Betty, Harry's wife. She was adoringly called Tanta Betty in Yiddish by family members, and Betsy by my close friends. She was the sweetest woman who possessed a heart of gold. She did not have a bad bone in her body. She was a private and introverted person. She loved people, but best and most of all she adored and worshiped my Uncle Harry. She somehow saw him as more than a handsome star-like matinee idol, but as a personal savior, her prince charming who rescued her from a difficult orphaned childhood. He gave her purpose, meaning and direction in life.

As a young teenager she was wooed early on by Harry, the man of her dreams, and she submitted to his every wish to please him. They married quickly, but never had any children.

I, being in close proximity to her at the hotel as a youthful pre-teenager, watched her work without ever having a complaint as a kitchen assistant to my Uncle Jack, as a salad lady, kitchen woman, pantry girl, and jack of all kitchen trades. She created her own coleslaw, pickled herring, lox and even washed glasses, silverware, pots and pans when needed. Soon, after my Uncle Jack became gravely ill, she took over his position as a workhorse doing the work of two people in being responsible for running the entire kitchen.

Tanta Betty was a tall, heavyset, big boned, round shouldered, plain looking, loving and affectionate, hearty and strong woman who could have lived and survived any ordeal on the frontier of any country in the world.

I came to love her as my mother away from home during the summer seasons. She took care of me as though I were her son. I loved and respected her with every fiber in my body.

It is for those reasons that I was more than upset when Tanta Betty, feeling depressed and despondent, cried and confided to me about her unhappiness. She told me she was heartbroken and wanted to die because Harry had a history of being in philandering relationships with other women during their long marriage. Currently he was having an affair with the hotel bookkeeper leaving Betty publicly humiliated in front of the hotel guests.

In strict confidence she poured her heart out to me, mentioning the pre-Woodbine tale of the candy store lady, the current hotel bookkeeper, and the first year's bellhop's divorced secretarial mother who spent her two weeks summer vacation and subsequent weekends at the hotel, not taking in the sun, gambling or eating herself silly, but instead sitting in the hotel's station wagon opposite Harry while he drove to town to run errands. Then they would mysteriously disappear for hours and occupy vacant hotel rooms in the town of Ellenville, New York for their afternoon liaisons.

Betty was crushed, betrayed, ashamed and embarrassed by Harry's histrionics. If all this was not bad enough, Betty was most aggravated about the rumors, innuendos and open-ended remarks made by guests and others thinking that the bookkeeper was Harry's wife, that Betty did not exist, or that Harry had no wife. This accounted for his passive-aggressive behavior to other women who approached and flirted with him for his attention and sexual favors.

Further complicating the situation, the bookkeeper, who had bankrolled Harry with money for the Woodbine Hotel's expansion and renovations, found out that Harry was cavorting with the bellhop's mother. During a fit of jealous rage, the bookkeeper had the *chutzpah* to tell Betty about her own affairs with Harry, but also to tell her that Harry was cheating on both of them with "that New York City bitch." She said, "she was only one of many in Harry's harem."

Tanta Betty asked me, what she should do in what became a sad real life soap opera situation. I responded saying that she did not have to idly stand by and do nothing about Harry's adulterous and flaunting behavior, that she had grounds to legally leave him. She then stopped crying for a moment and in a matter of fact way she said rhetorically, "What could I do? Where could I go? What would become of me? ...I just couldn't leave him. I still love him despite everything wrong he has ever done to me..." She was thinking of him and not of herself. She said, "I love him too much to hurt him. I couldn't bear living life without him. I will be with him to my dying day."

Quite a statement, I thought. I was speechless sitting smack in the midst of a major family squabble beyond the stretch of my imagination. My naiveté as a teenager was forever shattered. This was real life cut open and raw to the bone.

My perceptions of Uncle Harry and Aunt Betty were to quickly change. Harry's actions and Betty's responsive comments cut through the old façade. The deceptions of the past no longer held water. The new reality was now clearly out in the open, not only for the guests to see, but for our family members to experience. Now, as a family, we all had to deal with the truth.

It now became clearly evident that the admiration for my Uncle Harry, accompanied with his grandiose dreams and ideas were nothing more than empty pipe dreams. His transgressive actions spoke volumes about his true character, which not only openly indicted him to the public but also profoundly found him guilty in the eyes of Aunt Betty and myself. We all had to live with the consequences of these devastating acts.

What could I do, as her nephew, to attempt to mend Tanta Betty's hurting broken heart? I took it upon myself to do two things: to shore up her self esteem and deal with her humiliation to enhance her identity as a person. She had been embarrassed to be seen in public or to go to the hotel's social hall in the evenings because of her clothes, the way she looked and the fact that she was always exhausted from her work schedule from sunrise to sunset in the kitchen.

I made Betty, Betsy to my friends in the dining room and kitchen, the darling of the hotel. Our crew worked our butts off helping Betty in the kitchen to finish all of her chores so that we could all go to the social hall, make her the center of attention, dance and have fun with her in front of all the guests for them to see and recognize that she was much more than just Harry's wife.

Secondly, having a driver's license, I would make it a habit, for one night during each week, to secure from Harry the hotel's car and take Tanta Betty and some of the dining room staff to one of the two movie houses in Ellenville. Betty was grateful beyond belief to all of us for the consideration and care we gave her. Realistically, these actions were but a short term fix to this major dilemma.

Although Harry was guilty of a great many sins, no matter what they were, he seemed to always be forgiven and remained the dashing prince of his family.

My mother held fast in her loyalty to him, saying he was a good man who had been corrupted and ruined by whores, *kurvehs* as she called them in Yiddish, who openly prostituted themselves to him for their own pleasure and needs. His older sister never assessed any blame to Harry, he being absolved by her as an innocent creature, an example of the common double standard practiced in its day during the time of moral transition following World War II.

Nevertheless, Harry was always the center of attraction of the family. He relished attention and was the epitome of the self-made creative entrepreneurial hotelman. So it often seemed at first glance to those he met, especially for the first time. However convincing he was to the people in his world, he was not truly worldly. Not only was he a philanderer many times over, but also a con artist and a phony who skillfully tried to mask his inadequacies through his out of proportion rhetoric in conversation with others.

Harry had less than a 3rd grade night school education and could just about write his name and barely get through the headlines of the newspapers. He was privately mocked behind his back by many who saw through his veneer. He often made obvious foolish judgments and lost a great deal of money by making poor business transactions. Often he was taken advantage of as prey by others who had less scruples and were more opportunistic and ruthless than even he was. He suffered from an inflated ego, and a self-serving personality.

May truth be told, he was often privately embarrassed by his debt at the conclusion of each season. In some instances, I often made more money than he did at summer's end. He often had to be bailed out season after season by borrowing money and taking notes from various banks at exorbitant interest rates to keep the business from going under.

He often convinced my mother, his oldest sister, to get my Dad to lend him money which he never paid back to open the next season. My father reluctantly, but always, gave him a dole, a handout, every season to placate my mother. When my mother came to the hotel for a seasonal month's vacation my father always insisted on paying her complete bill. He wanted no indebtedness or favors of any kind from my Uncle Harry. Harry, on the other hand, had the *chutzpah* to brag about this arrangement to his customered guests, his relatives and friends, saying that even his sister paid her own way, turning it around in such a way for his own personal entrepeneurial gain.

Harry, as a hotelman, in his own way transformed me, and him as well in this environment. It became a defining moment for both of us because he had no children. I became, for Harry, by geography and necessity, a confidant and surrogate son. I was the unwritten, but inferred and loosely promised, heir apparent to the hotel in the future. As a result of my seasonal Woodbine experiences I even foolishly thought of Harry as my adoptive father. I wondered what I had become as a person at this clouded point in my life. As I prepared to become a hotel manager, I met my girlfriend Shirl which prompted me to reconsider my decision to do so.

I surmised that I had become a mountain rat not only working in the summers at my uncle's place, but taking those skills beyond the Jewish holidays by working in non-Kosher hotels in the Ellenville and New York Metropolitan area whenever I was off from college.

I had lost my innocence during my adolescence in the freedom of the Catskills releasing me from my sheltered home life in Brooklyn. I had become, by my own ingenuity, monetarily and psychologically semi-self sufficient, transformed by my Uncle Harry.

Harry did not particularly like my girlfriend Shirl for the two seasons she worked at the hotel as a counselor. He thought her to be lazy. He also said she was a *kochlefel*, Yiddish insulting slang for a busybody, or someone stirring up problems with a large cooking spoon.

Quite the contrary, she was a legitimate, intelligent college student, bright, pretty and worldly. Early on, she saw Harry for what he really was—a phony, egotistical, show off, loud mouth, dashing figure that opportunistically conned people, even myself, to lend him money and to pay homage to himself. Shirl was a teenager wise beyond her years. He inwardly feared her because she was educated and a threat to his overblown reputation and persona. I became disillusioned from following in my Uncle's footsteps.

Although Harry had many liabilities as a person and a businessman, he was nevertheless instrumental in my life. He defined himself by becoming the center of his own created world. I orbited that world and eventually became part of that creation. He, in his own selfish way, mostly made those he came in contact with feel more relevant and important as people as a result of his dreams, escapades and misadventures.

He transformed himself from fruitman, to fisher, to hotelman within his lifetime. On the surface, he looked to be a great success. In reality, for those who knew the real truth, he was a failure, deceiving himself and so many others along the way.

Willpower, work and World War II, along with some good luck, brought him to a higher level, a level he would never be prepared for, the odds being greatly stacked against him. His personal inadequacies and lack of education would ultimately haunt him forever and prevent him from becoming a topflight successful hotelman.

In the world that he wanted to be successful in he would never be adequately prepared for the challenge. He would ultimately be doomed to failure. Filleting a fish is one thing, being a successful hotel entrepreneur is quite another.

For me, dreams and risk taking will always be essential to human growth. However, I found that there are no short cuts to success. Taking poor risks often result in failure. Being in touch with reality, having an education and working hard leads to stability, growth and success. One thing is certain—the informal education I received at the Woodbine Hotel gave me an awareness to be better prepared for a life I had to make on my own.

***

Toward the end of my working tenure at the Woodbine Hotel, Tanta Betty was diagnosed with breast cancer. Five years after her mastectomy her condition spread to her lymph nodes and became terminal. I flew to Florida on a New Year's weekend with my mother where Betty lived with Harry in a stationary trailer park to bid her farewell. They moved there after they had sold the hotel for a meager pittance. She hardly recognized my mother and I and she died a day later.

A few years later when Harry himself lay dying in a hospital bed in the New York metropolitan area, I visited him for the last time after our relationship had long since dissolved.

I always had one question on my mind that I had never before asked him. "Why did you do what you did with other women for all those years that you were married to Betty?" I asked.

He said, "I always knew that someday you would ask me that question because I know how much you loved Betty." I surmised that he was prepared to answer when he quickly said, "I really couldn't help myself. There was always too much temptation around me. I did what I did."

I tried to be fair-minded and accept his answer at face value despite the fact that I dearly loved my Aunt Betty. However, in my early twenties I could not sanction that lame excuse. Even now, as a mature adult, I could only find some solace in thinking back to my youth when I was transported from the fish store to the bakery and was exposed to my own array of temptations in the good looking, good smelling pastry treats.

Quite possibly Harry had been overcome by the assortment of flirtatious women he liked and was exposed to, such as the Joan Crawford type—dark haired, long, thin legged, big busted women; or the fair haired blonde Betty Grable World War II pinup type. Maybe those conquests made him feel more powerful to feed his enormous ego and sexual appetite.

Whether for good or evil, Harry magically became the man-child, lured by temptation and his own narcissistic conceit to take advantage of these situations, never to apologize to the very end of his life, justifying himself, his infidelities and selfish instincts. Betty's poor self esteem and dependence on Harry became the free ticket Harry needed to become the cat's meow for all callers to share his plentiful bounty. By remaining true to her marriage vows Betty endured more self-inflicted pain from sharing Harry with others. This pain evolved into an acceptance of conditioned emotional abuse.

As I matured I tried to examine and evaluate the tragic family saga of Uncle Harry falling from grace as he aged who then often became somewhat religiously pious by going to temple to pray, possibly looking for individual repentance and redemption.

As for Tanta Betty, my favorite aunt that I loved dearly, she reluctantly accepted her husband's infidelities. Not only did I see her and my other relatives as they really were, for better or worse or any shade in between, but I began to see my own personal ambivalence about my aunt and uncle's complex relationship.

I came to realize that not all memories of past experiences are necessarily good, that many bad memories are often forgotten or are put on the backburner as lesser events because of their immense corporate hurt to the individuals involved. To be objective and truthful in those situations can be difficult and painful at any age.

Facing the reality within the reflections of that chipped, old, faded green dish from the 1920s would become the symbolic vehicle that triggered the memory of the story of not just the Woodbine Hotel, but my maturation from an adolescent to a teenager, and eventually to a young adult who was an eye-witness and participant to the tragic and defining drama of our family. The dish, like "the Chair," in its time, gave meaning and purpose to its time. In its own way, it was the downbeat for the overture in relating the saga of a portion of our family's history.

The two adult men in my life, when I was growing up, both rang true to themselves. The major differences between them and their impact upon me were that my Uncle Harry was a glamorous dreamer, a risk taker who tried to climb the ladder of success to reach the highest plateau during his lifetime, whereas my father was realistically accepting of his lot in life. He worked from "the Chair," satisfied as an honest, hard working, truthful tailor who grew and adapted in a similar way to the persons he serviced by mimicking the pattern of changing styles of clothing as the seasons changed.

***

Ironically, my father had the foresight and wisdom long before Harry's open liaisons with adventurous women to take a few matters into his own hands. My father made his lending money to Harry contingent upon a promise from Harry to commit to buying a family plot in my father's own *shtetl* cemetery. He required that Harry and Betty have a double stone to be perpetually cared for in eternity at the New Montefiore Cemetery in Suffolk County in eastern Long Island.

At that point, my father could not have foreseen what would happen after Betty's death. He could have no way of knowing that Harry would continue his affair with his bookkeeper until she had a stroke in Florida and was confined to a wheelchair.

The bookkeeper's very common younger, single sister, while taking care of her bedridden older sister until she died, was always envious of her sister's open relationship with Harry. She had always eyed and flirted with Harry when she visited the Hotel.

Now it was open season for acquiring Harry. He, being older and lonely, was fair game. They became a couple, went to Israel for vacation, got married there and returned to Florida until Harry got gravely sick and died in the New York metropolitan area. She gained not only her sister's inheritance, but also Harry and Betty's trailer.

When I was notified that Harry was on his deathbed, I saw him and asked him for my Uncle Jack's ring. It was originally a simple gold and black onyx that he wore next to his swollen finger. Harry had changed the ring to a cat's eye when he took it from Jack when he died. The ring and the dish remain for posterity.

"The Chair" and "The Dish" are the remnants of singular artifacts that link the past to the present. They symbolize the pathway and approach of common folks such as my father, my uncle and his wife, to survive, adapt and succeed from the arduous challenge of a foreign environment in Amerika.

Within their tales, my family members were trying to find and define their own method to achieve their purpose and way in life. Doing their deeds, in their own manner, paved the way for me growing up, learning from and absorbing their experiences, to look ahead and try to find my own destiny, thus attempting to bridge the cultural gap in my life span from the 20th to the 21st century.

Book II

The Cloud

One day a little boy went on a stroll through a garden. It was an exceptionally long garden and the more he walked the longer it seemed. He walked on and on endlessly, until he became confused and no longer knew where to walk.

He stopped and sat down for a moment on the soil beneath him and sighed deeply. He was out of breath and so very tired. As he rested and caught his breath, he noticed that it suddenly had become extremely dark. Not knowing why, he immediately looked up and noticed a dark cloud directly above him.

This was no ordinary cloud; it seemed to have some special quality; it seemed to be real, almost human. The more he looked at the cloud, the more he noticed its composition. He sat and wondered, not knowing whether to be frightened, whether to run, or to remain still.

The cloud seemed to have stopped moving and remained in the same position as the boy. The boy began to wonder why such a cloud, the likes of which he had never seen before, had stopped and remained perfectly still above his head. He remembered why he had come to the garden. Was not the garden somehow new and different from his common daily life? He felt an air of excitement just being there.

How happy he was to be away from the monotony of his friends and their silly games. He was truly bored at home, never knowing what to do or where to go to enjoy himself. His friends' games did not appeal to him, but nevertheless he went along and played for lack of some creativity on his own part.

He had not the type of personality to be a leader, for his voice was high like that of a woman, his figure thin, and his face undeveloped as most boys his age. He nevertheless played and in time began to feel contempt for himself and to even resent his very existence.

Realizing that playing with his friends was not what he wanted, he decided against playing that day and so wandered into the garden.

In his dreams he thought himself to be a prince decked in beautiful garments and sitting upon a white horse and when he would ride in full view of his friends, family, and subjects, they would become wild with joy. What honor, what beauty, he was their prince and they were his people. What a marvelous illusion it all was.

As he looked about he saw the reality that no one shared but him. He found that he was alone with a nakedness that no one could understand. Where and what are the pleasures of life, he asked himself.

He thought, thought, and thought some more. But the more he thought, the worse it became. He surely was not a mute, then why wasn't he understood?

The reality of life was unbearable. His family didn't give him the attention he wanted and his friends made fun of his appearance. So the little boy felt rejected, depressed, and blue. He had absolutely no one he could go to and in his misery he thought of things other than games. He thought of nature, the flowers, the birds, the trees, the moon, sun and stars. These things given without prejudice were his substitute and escape.

Although he believed himself ugly, he knew his eyes were jewels that could give him pleasure by the sight of such things. This simple pleasure could empty his heart of all the misery and sorrow that he felt for himself. In observing the items that he enjoyed with his eyes, he had never included the clouds. He seemed to take them for granted, after all there were oh so many of them.

Now that one was above his head, he wondered why he had never before appreciated the clouds. This cloud seemed like the king of all clouds. There was an air of mystery about it. It was dark and seemed to be breathing almost like a human. As its breath became stronger the cloud became darker until it was as dark as night. The little boy looked about, saw it wasn't night and began to run. As he ran, the cloud followed him with its breath becoming stronger. The little boy ran until he was out of breath, and fell wearily to the ground. As he fell, the cloud stopped its movement. The little boy yelled to the cloud, "Why are you following me? Who are you great cloud? What do you want of me?" With this the little boy began to cry like he never cried before. He was so very afraid. He cried for his mother and father, his friends, but all in vain. He knew as he cried out that no one would hear him, that he was isolated from everything, that it was he and the cloud. With this he wondered whether the cloud would kill him, whether his life would end. "Why not," he said to himself. "Let the cloud kill me, no one cares about me, what difference would it make it I live or die, I might be better off dead, that way I wouldn't be in anyone's way. My friends wouldn't have to lend me toys to play with. I wouldn't have to look at myself in the mirror, why not!"

So his decision was made. If the cloud wanted to kill him, then he would be willing. Now, not having anything to fear, he rose from the ground, wiped his eyes, and looked directly up at the cloud and yelled, "I'm not afraid of you cloud!"

With this there was a tremendous roar of thunder, the likes of which the boy had never heard. His head felt as if it were shattered and again he fell to the ground. This time he noticed the cloud had become even darker. He had never seen such darkness before. Suddenly, after the cloud opened itself, it began to rain. But this was no ordinary rain; it was as if needles were piercing his body. This little boy screamed as the rain drops covered him and began to come down with even more intensity.

The little boy was in terrible pain and yet he was not afraid, even of death. He rose once more and looked at the cloud and said, "I have no fear of you cloud, I am strong, your rain gives me pain but I can endure you cloud."

The cloud darkened even more and more rain descended. The boy stood firm in his tracks feeling its pain and then the rain began to let up until it stopped. The boy looked up and saw the cloud become lighter and lighter and saw the north wind come and blow the cloud away. The boy looked at himself and felt his body, he was alive and breathing, he had surely won the battle with the cloud. He went home feeling strong and healthy. He was now truly a warrior.

Becky's Boy

I was born into a world that was self-contained within the two block radius around the Jewish Community House, or the JCH, of Bensonhurst, at Bay Parkway and 78th Street in New York City. My home was at 2118-76th Street in the Bensonhurst section of Brooklyn. I lived there for the next twenty-two years of my life.

I entered this world in a building diagonally across from the JCH that was a singular ground floor building, never classified as a hospital, but as a maternity ward for birthing babies. Later, that same housing was transformed into a small old age residence, as the inhabitants of the neighborhood began to age with the passing of time.

I was always puzzled by the fact that I was named Sidney. It was only one of many questions that bothered me as a child. Another concern I had was simply because my mother was prematurely gray. I always remembered her as an older woman. I often speculated and wondered if, in fact, I was even her son. I thought that I might have possibly been adopted.

It is only through looking at some early baby pictures with my mother that I actually began to believe I was definitely her son. Therefore, it became my contention that my name, Sidney, was selected and given to me by the obstetrician. I always questioned how my mother could have ever come up with the name Sidney.

The doctor, who I logically believed must have been Jewish, was told by my parents that my given name was "*Shmiel Moisha*" in Yiddish, and "*Schmiel Moshe*" in Hebrew. Apparently he translated the name in English to be Sidney Morris or Sidney Murray. However, in the naming confusion and excitement, the name Sidney Moe appeared on my birth certificate. This name, at least according to me, never seemed to suit my personality. Eventually, as I got older and matured, I began to drop the "ney" of Sidney and settled on being called just plain Sid. I never ever used the name Moe, and therefore completely discarded it. For most of my life I have been called Sid, except by my parents and my early childhood friends who always knew me as Sidney.

My family name of Winter can be tied with research to the ancient linguistic term "vinter," defined as a wine maker. My father, as it turns out, did know how to distill wine and did so in our basement. I loved my last name, but hated the season. I, like my mother, always felt cold, chilled to the bone and deplored wearing lots of clothing while experiencing the winter blahs and blues. My father, on the other hand, loved walking in the cold, white and fresh snow that gleamed on the ground, with winter winds blowing while expelling his visibly warm breath into the frigid air.

It was during the first week in April, in the year 2008, when spring is supposed to burst forth from its hibernation, that I was suddenly aware that the spring rains teeming from the skies were reminiscent of those from my youth, which were an extension of a lingering reminder of the long, cold, winters of my childhood discontents. Today's horizontal winds were continuously blowing cold with piercing, heavy raindrops the size of quarters spitting out of the heavens like spiny porcupine needles. The waters of this new season were deep and dingy, discoloring the ground and making it impossible to set foot on the earth outside of my home without fisherman's boots. I felt as if I were a prisoner, anchored in stone as if in Noah's ark being shut in my solitary abode, unable to take my habitual daily walk in the adjacent woods.

More importantly, the rains reminded me of an unbelievably dark and dreary day in my childhood when my mother picked me up from my elementary school. She arrived lugging a large umbrella, my oversized rubbers and raincoat, to affectionately take home her little *Zindele* (son in Yiddish), on a dreadful day of weather some 67 years ago in the year 1941.

My mother, may she rest in peace, was the quintessential Jewish mother. She was the ultimate worrier.

I remember her concern, bordering on an obsession, with my health. She had grown up in a society with a very high infant mortality rate, and had seen many friends and relatives in Russian Poland succumb to various childhood illnesses and die. Whenever I became ill as a child my mother became extremely terrified, and tried to allay my own fears about illnesses. Nevertheless, I was constantly frightened as a child.

Then and forever I was called her *Zindele*, her only son who was very precious to her. I was the love of her life, her *boy-chikel*, Yiddish for her little boy, her gift to her immediate family and her validation as a woman. There is no question in my mind that in an authoritarian world mostly manipulated by ego driven men and women, her coming to school to pick me up in a severe spring storm was a good deed, a *mitzvah* that any well intentioned mother would do for her one and only son. She, in every way, was true to this endearing task.

However, for me, I was embarrassed and ashamed, being too consumed with myself and my own insecurities to understand her altruistic actions. While my mother was concerned and protective of me, my response was one of feeling small, weak and thoroughly dependent on her. As if things weren't bad enough for me to digest, in my own childish judgment I felt even more inadequate simply because most of the mothers came to school to pick up their little daughters. I stood out, being the only male to be picked up by their mother. For the males in our class, it was an accepted honor to walk home in the rain, like a grown up. Being picked up was a humiliation and further affirmed my complete dependency on my mother in what, for me, was a major crisis.

I felt like the smallest insect, a sissy, who had just been emasculated for all to see. As we walked home, my tears were mixed with the spring rains. I will never forget that experience. That was the last time my mother ever picked me up from school to take me home. From that early experience she and I began to realize who I was and how I felt as a young and sensitive person in a new school.

Like a chain reaction I began to recollect going to kindergarten for the first time in my neighborhood elementary school. My mother had taken me to school that first day. I felt ill at ease, as if I did not belong there. I was assured by my mother that everything would be fine. When she left me I was in a virtual state of panic. I felt as tight as a drum but tried to suppress my feelings within my mind and body.

I couldn't believe my eyes when the teacher gathered us together in the schoolyard as a group that had to line up according to size. I was amazed to find that two boys were in front of me in line. This made me feel as if I were not alone in the world, that there were people as thin, small and short as I.

My luck quickly ran out as most of the clothing that I wore in elementary school consisted of hand-me-downs that my father had picked up working in his various tailoring jobs at cleaning stores. He would alter these garments to fit me. Most often the clothes were very heavy, uncomfortable, and itchy customer discards. To this day I never wear heavy woolen clothes, as I was always self-conscious feeling itchy and scratching myself in various places, especially in the crotch, as a child.

One day I wore leggings, or overalls, that my mother pronounced as "roveralls," in Kindergarten. They had clasps which had to be undone to relieve oneself. Because I had to go to the bathroom I tried but could not undo the buckles. Too nervous, embarrassed and frightened to even ask for help, I made in my pants. This was a catastrophe that I had to live with in my mind. Life in school at that point in time was anything but rewarding.

However the worst was yet to come for my mother and me when she was summoned to come to school to see the assistant principal, Miss Fitzgerald.

Fritzy, a spinster as she was called in private among the students, was a tall, grey-haired, overweight, overbearing, pear-shaped authoritarian woman responsible for running the school. She was fiercely outspoken and threatening in her demeanor. You always knew when she was coming into view from her bellicose and brazen speech, but also by her heavy steps that sounded like thunderclaps coming from the sky. She sported a short, butch haircut brushed back, similar to an army crew cut. She had a small head and piercing eyes. She seemed to have only one faded blue, ancient dress, along with a thick belt that she always wore as her uniform.

Her matronly pot-bellied torso was adorned with a long lasso-like silver chain that, when extended, reached the floor. It held the school's keys and her ever-present whistle. She somehow mastered using the chain and whistle in such a way that a cowboy might lasso a calf in a rodeo, or a fisherman casting a line in the water. She was a whiz at spinning the chain and winding it around her arm and then releasing it like the punctuated, vipered fangs of a snake. To say that she was intimidating to the student, staff and parents was a gross understatement. She was feared as if she were the multi-faceted inquisitorial police and judge combined. She was a product of a parochial school environment run strictly by nuns. She, having been exposed to that system, found her niche in life in the New York City school system and relished her position of power and intimidation in our neighborhood school in Bensonhurst, Brooklyn.

Little did my mother know what was in store for her in the meeting to come with Miss Fitzgerald. My mother was asked to come to school because I had not conformed to the assembly day dress code of a white dress shirt, dark pants, and a red tie.

My mother, always being protective of her only son, would dress me with flannel shirts when I went to school. She was fearful that with the drafts in the school building and exposure to other children during the winter season I would be susceptible to becoming sick. I had been sickly since early childhood on, and had often suffered from sinus infections and respiratory illness.

During assembly, held once a week, I was sent to the back of the auditorium along with other students who violated the dress code. As the weeks went on, I became the only child who did not conform to the dress code. Although I had told my mother, she couldn't and wouldn't believe that the school would not make an exception to this rule because I was prone to catching colds. My father agreed, saying that they would understand the situation in *Amerika*. Hence, a letter was sent, and the meeting with Miss Fitzgerald was made.

My mother was at a distinct disadvantage in this situation. She was ill-prepared, as many often were, when taken to Fritzy. She did not understand the rules of the school. Not knowing the English language, she could not communicate on any level with Miss Fitzgerald. An interpreter was brought in to explain the school rules, what was required and where certain items could be bought. My mother was embarrassed and ashamed, and felt out of place as she herself was not properly dressed. However, the hatchet job belonged to

Fritzy, who used my mother as a pin cushion for her vindictive and demeaning remarks. Her tone was that resembling the Nazi Gestapo.

I sat there in the office, frozen-faced, seeing my mother take blow after blow, literally being victimized and dissected as a functional illiterate green-horned person. I felt helpless as she anguished over the horrendous experience. She had gone to school in a well-intentioned, good-mannered way to resolve a problem (mine and hers), but the results were devastating.

It is no wonder that my mother was forever more too embarrassed and ashamed to ever set foot in that school or any other school again. Not only did I tell her not to pick me up from school anymore, but my mother seemed to agree with this now. I hated Fritzy with a passion, but I was captive in that school until I graduated some five years later.

The next day we went to the dry goods store and bought the white shirt and red tie. Although I felt very angry and school phobic at times, I forced myself to always attend no matter how I felt. I no longer was ostracized to the back of the auditorium and became a school conformist. I even took part in a stage production of "March of the Wooden Soldiers" as a toy wooden soldier.

Being vindictive to the core, Miss Fitzgerald sent a directive to my teacher to immediately take me out of my regular class and placed me in the "special class" near the basement of the school. I was labeled and classified as a student who had a foreign accent. She had noticed in our meeting that my mother spoke to me exclusively in Yiddish and that I responded accordingly in Yiddish.

The "special class," as it was formally called then, was comprised of disadvantaged and disabled children of all ages with all types of learning, physical and medical problems.

Within the school, this class was shunned and given the name by regular students as "the crippled class."

Upon entering the class, I immediately noticed a boy about three years older than I with blue lips and blue fingers. Another boy who was overweight had a frozen wrist bent towards his own body; he walked with a severe limp and dragged his foot. Others there squinted through thick glasses while others had speaking and hearing problems. Many looked sickly with red eyes and yellowish skin coloring.

This was the all purpose room meant to hide all the misfits of the school. I learned a great deal from this experience. Being in that environment I felt worse than ever, always praying to be saved but wanting to die. Was I being punished by Fritzy because she hated my mother and me for being first generation Jewish immigrants? Was this her way of getting back at us for not following the mandates of the school? Or was it really for the teacher to work with me to try and improve my English language problem in school? In my confused state I couldn't figure out the reason that I had been dealt this prison sentence, for what became one week in hell.

I worked hard for that entire week to block out everything in my mind, concentrating only on improving my English. Finally, the next week my prayers were answered and I was put back in my regular class, feeling as though I had died and miraculously gone to heaven. The residual effect of this trauma was that from that moment on I would always speak to my mother and father in English, while she and my dad always communicated with me in Yiddish.

However, towards the end of that term, one of the most traumatic events I ever experienced in my life took place at that elementary school. It was the school administered audiometer test given for the first time to check our hearing. In the process of executing the exam, the students were seated in every other row, one seat behind another. In between the rows, a large wooden box was placed in the middle of the unoccupied row. Wires sprouted from the box like an octopus' tentacles in various directions. Attached to these wires were earphones. I was given a form with blank boxes, a pencil and an assigned seat. Once the test began, students were supposed to write down the numbers they heard on their form. The results would be checked to see if their hearing was satisfactory, or whether there was some hearing loss involved. As a young, frightened child this experience was overbearing, overwhelming and unforgettable.

I remember the test as if it were yesterday. In the headphones I heard the following statement: "Please write the numbers that you hear in the first column of your paper. Four-two, three-six, one-eight, two-five, one-three..." The sound level gradually became a lower decibel as the numbers went on, and then the process would repeat: "Please write the numbers that you hear in the second column of your paper."

As I observed the children in the class, they all wrote numbers down immediately in a staccato cadence. As the numbers got lower in volume, there was less writing and less scratching until there was no writing at all. Then, "Please write the numbers that you hear in the third column of your paper." The students began to write again. I happened to have heard nothing more through the rest of the exam and wrote nothing down, turning in a blank paper. I internally panicked to the point where tears began to flow down my face. Being as frightened as I was, I was unable to explain what happened. I thought I was a sickly child going deaf.

As a result of the failed audiometer test, I again was placed in the special class of students of all types of physical and mental maladies. I remained there for yet another week until the school decided to retest students who had failed the audiometer test. I think the happiest moment, at least at that point in my life, occurred when they found out the machine that was attached to my headphones during the first exam was defective as a result of an electrical short. When given the test again I was so excited when I heard the numbers loud and clear that I broke my pencil point. This time I excitedly raised my hand, stood up and demanded that I get another pencil. I was overjoyed then, and knew that I was a normal hearing child. I was immediately returned to my correct class. I felt a wave of relief and was pleased to be back in my regular class. Having been placed in the special class bothered me to no end and I never forgot that experience for the rest of my life.

***

The reality of the Americanization of Becky Winter, my mother, was slow to develop in *Amerika*. The awful truth was that she experienced a plague of problems in many areas of her life because of her inadequacies with the English language and adjusting to American culture. Therefore, because of her short-falls, she became frustrated and extremely dependent on my sister, my father and myself.

However, with time on her side and her secure home as her castle and comfort zone, she endured and gradually grew in her own style and way in the neighborhood that had become her personal domain.

Like most women of the 1940s and 1950s generation, my mother was strictly a housewife. A short while after marrying my father, she became pregnant with my sister, Helen. The pregnancy and birth were quite difficult for her so she abstained from having another child for five years. It was always my personal belief that my mother might have settled for having only one child if Helen had been born a male.

My mother traditionally shopped, cooked, cleaned and ran our household, although cleaning became her obsessive and compulsive forte. The rules of the house were strict whereby certain rooms were declared off limits by my mother resulting in my spending little or no time in certain sections of the house, especially the living room, dining room and sun parlor. Most of the time I was confined to the kitchen and the adjacent kitchenette or the bedroom that I shared with my sister Helen at a very young age.

Becky Winter accepted her lot in life and learned from her experiences. She adapted and began to overcome her short-comings by frequenting local stores on her own, buying everything she needed to sustain our home life during the week. She was only dependent on my father to help her on Sundays when he was sometimes off work and could do the heavy lifting when buying bottles of prune juice and awkward heavy items needed at home. My father also became her enabler and knight protector, taking her shopping for dresses, shoes, eyeglasses and anything else in neighborhoods unfamiliar to her in New York City.

Once she became proficient understanding U.S. currency, she became prudent in saving silver dollars, half dollars and quarters in large, glass jars that she secured in the many closets in our house. She continuously saved the change from the cash allowance that my father gave her weekly to run the house.

My mother could not read or write. She was a functional illiterate. Every year my sister, at first, and then I would prepare and submit alien papers to the United States government so that she would not risk being deported to the old country. We spent hours trying to show her how to write her name. It was imperative and necessary for her to be at least able to write her signature on various legal documents. This was always a chore, and in the end she would always laugh at her own difficulty in a self-depreciating manner due to the fact that she had to be guided in every way. She never wrote her name the same way whenever she signed a document. Nevertheless, she was a bright and emotional woman. Ten years before she died she became a citizen of the United States of America. This came about because my father knew someone who would accept her oral response to the questionnaire. Even though she was handicapped literally, she became politically astute and acquired a great deal of knowledge of what was happening in the world from what she heard on the radio.

Her outlet to the world was the radio, one radio station in particular, WEVD, which broadcast many of their programs in Yiddish at certain times of the day on a very weak signal band. My mother would religiously listen to the transcribed radio shows and learn a great deal not only from the news broadcasts, but also about people's lives in *Amerika*.

One of the personalities she would listen to was the Yiddish *philosof*, or Jewish philosopher, who received letters and commentaries from people about personal conflicts in their lives. They asked him questions about how to resolve those difficult problems. He would address those issues and, like a psychologist, would formulate an answer that he felt was fair-minded and acceptable to the parties involved. From his responses my mother gained invaluable amounts of knowledge about moral behavior and life in *Amerika*. Furthermore, she learned about the New York City Yiddish culture and history, which was quite prevalent in the 1920s and 1930s. WEVD would also present current stories, dramatic classics, soap operas and musical interludes featuring artists of the Yiddish stage. That radio station became her informal educational lifeline beyond the neighborhood to the outside world.

During the high holy days my parents attended services. Because my mother was slow in reading from the formal Hebrew siddur, she never finished any passage that she read at the services. However, she would always pluck away and do the best that she could despite knowing her own limitations in the synagogue.

Although being the last on our block to get a television set, when we did get one, my mother fully enjoyed watching professional wrestling hosted by Dennis James, featuring an assortment of good and bad guys. As a teenager, I always saw my mother watching wrestling on the TV venting her vehement temper tirades directed at the recognizable villains.

My mother further expanded her horizons by consenting to go with my sister, Helen, to the neighborhood motion picture shows. The motivation for my mother to go to the movies was driven by the complementary free dish that was given every paid patron on a designated night in the middle of each consecutive week. Each week one dish was given towards the completion of a full fine china set that was displayed beautifully in the front lobby of the theater.

From visiting the theater, my mother was further acclimated to the English language. She was also exposed to Hollywood with its gallery of movie stars such as Joan Crawford, Bette Davis and Barbara Stanwyck, whom my mother always called Barbara Stanley.

Upon occasion, when my sister was unable to attend the showings, my mother would take me along to the movies. The experience was an educational one for me as well.

I looked about the theater and saw that every seat was occupied and that I was the only male of any age in attendance except for the movie projectionist. The women, of all ages, were all holding their free dish close to their hearts in a protective way throughout the film. My mother, always prepared for the occasion, brought three brown shopping bags placed inside the other to protect her valuable dish. The dishes themselves were adorned with flowered patterns in different arrangements and colors. However, the movie patrons had to attend from three to six months to complete the entire set.

Once the film began there was complete silence in the theater, as the female customers watched intently, usually observing the melodramatic acting skills of the female leads. Then, as if from nowhere, a dish would fall to the hard concrete floor and shatter into pieces. At that precise moment the ladies in the audience could not restrain themselves and, en masse, broke out in uproarious laughter and applause as if they were at a live sporting event.

At first I was frightened and very much surprised, never having seen or heard anything like that in my young life. When I looked at my mother and saw her response, I was equally taken aback that she, too, was contributing—not by yelling, but by clapping her hands in polite applause. The film continued as if nothing ever happened until the next predictable dish disaster. This happened at least five times every time I was present at the Benson Theater showings.

Sometimes if people came late to the movie house there were no more dishes to be awarded. Other times vouchers were given out if there were special dishes of the set to be given to the customers. My mother was upset upon receiving a piece of paper instead of a dish, having to return to the theater two or three times to get the special serving dishes. They were difficult to attain and, as a result, we never completed a full set of china. To this day, I have saved all those old dishes in my mother's dining room breakfront as mementos of that special time.

However, my mother attended as best she could and as a result was exposed to the new and contemporary American culture. Most of the films she disliked, saying that the female movie stars did not appear real with their painted faces, their overacting and, as she expressed in Yiddish, *pishen mit de oigen*, pissing with the eyes.

In her own way, my mother became the live movie star and center of attraction in our family. She overcame her language frustrations by not only speaking and cursing in Yiddish on the telephone with relatives, but also by acting out in our family conversations. My mother was not at all an angelic personality. Rather, she recoiled from society, becoming a reclusive and less than proactive person in the real world.

Instead, she lashed out and vented her feelings from her self-made safe and convenient world at home. The world she criticized included targeting my sister and my father, as well as the people she disliked on her radio shows. In addition, her enemies included villainous wrestlers on television, the obsessive rich and the politically unjust.

She became very opinionated, openly disliking a great many people, except for one person—me, because in her eyes I was always special. This was so much so that she went out of her way to buy me an endless supply of any foods that I liked, such as Yankee Doodles, Devil Dogs, cupcakes and éclairs. I could do no wrong in her eyes.

Then one day, as a second-grader, it was obvious to my mother that I was mired in melancholy and loneliness. She approached me, put both of her hands on my shoulders and looked directly into my eyes. She said, "One day, someday, my son, you will be great." I noticed that there were tears in her eyes as she uttered these words to me, her bewildered and uncomprehending son. My immediate impression was that of being stunned, confused and taken aback by her remarks. I wondered what she meant by her statement or if, in fact, she even understood what she had just said.

Being too young and naïve to even seriously understand what had just happened, I shrugged off what I felt were silly sayings and buried them somewhere in the recesses of my mind. I refused to think that it was anything more than my mother being empathetic, as any mother would be, to her moody, immature and needy son. At best I looked at it as a false hope, fools gold offered to placate her sad little child.

That incident by itself normally would have been forgotten, but for me (unknown to me at that time), that statement became a profound and meaningful commentary throughout my life. I was never to forget the statement or the emotional look and meaning in my mother's water drenched eyes. The bitter tears she shed made her remark more than just propaganda, but rather an honest reassurance and wish from her heart and soul for her son to triumph in life.

Her simple statement was not the saying of a sacrosanct sage, or just a mother's communication with her son, but rather an overriding belief in her boy. It was then, at that precious defining moment, that I became Becky's Boy.

Her words became her lament and credo when she spoke to me, repeated to me again and again at the difficult times in my life. As I matured to adulthood it became an invisible banner for me to race towards, as her words were etched in my brain for me to carry through my efforts and travails in life. It became my quest, as little boy lost in his own mind, and locked in his own house, to one day try to become somebody.

There is no realistic way of knowing exactly what my mother meant by saying, "One day, someday, my son, you will be great." I can only come away thinking that her expression of love, inspiration, empathy and belief on my behalf became a beacon for me, like a brilliant illuminated path shining from a lighthouse, lighting the way to the apex of a mountaintop.

Striving to please my mother, even long after she died, is still very much a part of my life. My accomplishments have linked me with her dreams in reality, for all time making me Becky's Boy.

Sam's Son

During my childhood, my mother always referred to me kindly as her boy when speaking to others, whereas my father always spoke of me proudly as his son. Hence, the name of this piece is entitled "Sam's Son."

My parents were as different as night and day. They were so opposite as people and personalities that I often wondered why they were married to one another. My mother, a robust extrovert, was attractive and pretty-looking whereas my father was somewhat plain with simple features. My father was deeply sensitive, bright, intelligent, introverted, withdrawn and laid back. My mother was talkative, extroverted, outwardly emotional and a charmer.

My father was almost Nordic in appearance. He had milk white skin, hairless in body, straight blond hair tinged with red highlights and exceedingly sensitive pure light blue eyes. If left out in the sun even for five minutes he would get a beet red sunburn, so he avoided it whenever possible. My mother, on the other hand, loved the sun and loved tanning her body.

With all their qualities combined as one, they could claim to make a whole, vibrant, and very functional personality. Separately, however, they were somewhat deficient and seemed out of sorts and out of place in America to the eyes of their young son.

She was the hospitable housewife who never worked for wages one day in her lifetime in America; and he was the consummate work beast and provider, never missing a day of labor from illness during his working life.

My mother inherited the terrible "Tenner tantrums" from her father, Max Tenner. He was the primadon of his family and either faked or actually suffered from epileptic seizures. He exploited this malady to get his way and garner attention from within his immediate family. My mother, an actor in her own right, copied the same mannerisms and replicated these actions to a fault, becoming another attention seeker and empowering her to be the dictator of our household.

At times, this was very frightening for me to see as a young child. No matter, these displays were quite effective and would quell our immediate family at the pass if we made an opposing argument that rubbed my mother the wrong way. My father became afraid of such displays and always placated my mother not to aggravate her.

My mother followed in her father's footsteps in how he set an example of succinctly showing her the way to gain control in our family.

My grandfather Max, *Maylech* in Yiddish, came to America,

worked five hard years, saved enough money and brought his wife and children to a foreign promised land. From that time on he never worked another day in his life. Early on, he proclaimed his retirement and demanded to be supported by his two sons for the duration of his life. He felt that his children, especially his sons, should be indebted to him for the rest of his lifetime for giving them the opportunity not only to escape the Russian Army, but also to live the "good life" in a new country.

Dad was quite internally emotional as a result of his stuttering speech impediment. He would often shed tears whenever he felt any pangs of emotion, whereas my mother rarely ever cried. His words were measured because he could only handle a few at any given time due to his self-consciousness about his speech. He actually spoke with his impressive eyes, showing his true intensity and emotions.

He was gentle, passive, reassuring, and a dependable voice in our house. His word was his badge of honor and the voice of reason and rationality in our home, rather than my mother's voice which bordered on the sound of dramatic theatrics.

He never cursed or expressed his temper in any out of control manner. He, in my judgment, never had a bad bone in his body. Generally, he didn't speak ill of people. Nearly all his peers, workers, friends and relatives never gave him a bad word.

His philosophy was more than shaped by experiencing not only social discrimination in Russian Poland, but also from the full blown Depression in the late 1920s and early1930s in America.

He became prudent, sometimes even frugal to a fault, and

hated to spend money unwisely on foolish things, *narishkiten* in Yiddish. He embraced the notion of saving for a rainy day. He was fearful of the capitalistic economic system, which he felt had become a perverted moneyed society based on greed, inequality and exploitation of workers in America.

As a Jew, he was sensitive as a result of his anti-Semitic experiences in the old world.

Ironically, it was America that became the land that he loved—it was the same capitalistic system that he often criticized that afforded him the opportunity to not only become an American citizen belonging to a free and democratic country, but to rise in station as a result of his personal work ethic. He was willing to sacrifice the purchase of needless material items. By so doing he would hoard funds for emergencies. He successfully saved money as a common laborer despite the capitalist system, which he felt heavily favored the entrepreneurial and upper classes.

This became his political and economic philosophy for the duration of his 76 years of life. He tried to instill these ideas into me, his only son.

My father was a privately confirmed agnostic as a result of his indirect involvement with the Holocaust. His entire family, which remained in his European home *shtetl* called Sochachov in Poland, was liquidated during WWII. When I, as a young child, meekly asked him, "Daddy, do you believe in G-d?"

He said, "I would like to very much, but I can't because my family was murdered by the Nazis."

Then he said, "There is no G-d, if so many terrible things can happen to millions of good people."

Nevertheless, he respected the faith of his birth and partici-pated in observing the High Holy Days, perhaps fearful of the possibility of there actually being a G-d. It became apparent to me as a pre-teen that having respect for G-d and his faith was simply secondary to pleasing and patronizing my mother who kept the faith until my father died. It was then that she became quite angry at G-d. She said, "G-d has taken my husband away from me at the time of my life when I needed him the most in order to help take care of me." Her temper had become fully directed at G-d. Her direct response was that she no longer would attend any services in the synagogue or celebrate reli-gious holidays.

Prior to that time she had always been a religious participant as a very devout Orthodox Jew, lighting candles every Friday evening and observing the holidays in a very strict manner. However, my mother never took to wearing a *sheitel*, a wig over her head.

By living about two miles from where her parents lived, my mother could be flexible and independent and sometimes bent the rules concerning her religion to suit her needs. The ground rules for the family were for us to walk about a mile and a half to go to her father's *shul* and pray during the high holy holi-days, especially *Yom Kippur*, which was designated in the faith as a fasting day.

But because I was a sickly child, I was given special permis-sion by my doctor and the hospital Rabbi to eat on Yom Kippur. On that special day, I had the greatest appetite in my life because I knew that I was different and could eat at the *shul* while everyone else was fasting. My father fully supported my mother and approved these medical decisions despite objections from others in religious circles. For my parents, anything to get me to eat something at that difficult time in my life was acceptable. That something was delicious chicken salad sandwiches, which I loved to eat, made by my mother only for me on those memorable days.

As an impressionable pre-kindergarten little boy, I would, on occasion, stay up late to see my father when he would come home late from work. He would eat his dinners with my mother and perform what became a magical act for me. I would get great pleasure from watching him "turn the clock," a green Session clock which he had purchased in the lower east side of Manhattan. It had a painted picture of a boat on the bottom portion of clock. Above, on the face of the clock were holes to insert the key which had to be hand turned. My father would have to stand on a chair and turn the key. I always loved too see and hear the sound of the winding of the key that he made when he turned the clock, or *zaiquer* as he called it in Yiddish. To this day, I still have this memento which was so comforting, assuring and meaningful in the memories it had always evoked in my young life.

For me, the clock became an animate material thing, almost human-like in nature, as if its ticks and pendulum swings were human heart beats. It was my father's creation. If the key wasn't wound, it wouldn't live. My father gave it life every day. He was a magician. Today, it is an antique, my own personal museum piece.

One day when I was a pre-teen, as a birthday gift, my sister gave me a beautiful pair of new genuine brown leather fur-lined gloves. At that time, it was the best birthday gift I had ever received. I couldn't wait for it to snow so I could go out and play with my warm fur-lined leather gloves, which would surely keep my hands nice and warm while I played and made snowballs.

The next day, as if G-d had planned it, it began to snow. I went outside and fully enjoyed a snowball fight on that unusual winter day. When I entered the house, I was completely covered with snow. I was soaked from head to toe: my shoes, my socks, my feet, even my pants and my jacket. After I took off my soaked shoes and socks, I took off my gloves and put them on the radiator to dry out.

My mother was cleaning the house at that time and did not see or hear me enter the house. When she finally returned to our kitchenette and saw me sitting there in my underwear with wet clothing all about the floor she was furious. She displayed her rage in the typical Tenner Temper Tantrum fashion, like a volcano about to erupt. She became overwrought and began cursing to no end. She picked up one of my waterlogged shoes, now twice its regular weight and threw it at me. The shoe only hit my left little pinky toe, but the blow still gave me great pain. I controlled myself by biting my lip and not crying out.

Her tirade went on and on until a strange, unfamiliar smell began to permeate the house. She was so caught up in her angry venting that she didn't realize that there was a foul smell. The smell was coming from my gloves on the radiator, which not only had dried out, but had shrunk a size smaller so that I could never use them again.

My mother was livid when she realized what had happened. "Just wait until your father comes home," she repeated again and again, rising in temper. *"Just wait until your father comes home!"*

I was terrified wondering what would happen later that evening.

When my father came home, I was in a panic. My mother, being hysterical, made a tremendous issue of the incident. "Punish him by giving him the strap," she said to my father. My father held fast, saying, "no," with tears in his eyes. But my mother prevailed as she reiterated, "teach him a lesson once and for all to behave in a proper manner, to never do these things again."

My father knew she would not stop her harangue and reluctantly said, "Ok., I'll do it." He had unwillingly consented to punishing me and walked into the bedroom where I was hiding. He quietly said to me under his breath, "Just stay behind the bed while I hit my belt to the floor and then scream out."

And that was all he did. He never hit me then, or ever during my entire life. My father could never do such a thing as to beat his own son whom he loved dearly. It was beyond his moral principles. He was truly in my eyes, a good Sam, a great Dadee.

My mother was the overseer of our house on the ground floor where we lived because she was always home and my father was mostly working, so by default my Dad's domain in our house became "the cellar."

The cellar was quite dark, drafty, damp, and totally unfriendly. It had pull string electrical sockets lodged into the ceiling which housed a few remote low watt light bulbs which gave minimum light through the large area beneath our ground floor apartment.

To one side of the basement were outcoves, or bins, which my father called *kamas*. It was in those *kamas* that my father reigned supreme.

In the largest *kama* there was an area way window which opened into our side alley way. That *kama* was closest to the large furnace of our house. By the joint ownership agreement with his older brother Joe who occupied the upstairs flat of the house, it was my father's responsibility to feed or stoke the furnace with coal to provide heat during the cold winter season. He was also responsible for cleaning up and removing the ashes from the furnace and cart them into the street for garbage collection.

Being a precocious kid, I would always trail after my father on Sundays, constantly asking questions such as, "Why do you go down into the cellar and disappear for so long?" and "What are the frightening noises I hear during the week that are like thunder claps?"

My father finally said, "Would you like to see what I do in the cellar?"

"Sure," I responded.

When I looked into the large *kama* I could only see the top of the ceiling and nothing else. The *kama* was filled with blue-black shiny rocks that glittered in the beams of light coming through the cracks at the top of the area way window. There was no door on this *kama*, but only a very wide opening. My father said, "The noises you hear at night are me shoveling coal into the furnace or taking the ashes out from below it."

I asked about the rocks. My father replied, "Those are special rocks that they call coal."

"Why is it blue-black?"

"There are different kinds of coal. Some are harder, some softer."

"I don't understand," I said.

"The harder the coal, the longer it burns and the more heat it gives off. It's also the most expensive coal, but it's the best because it lasts longer. They call it blue coal, that's what we use, it shines blue."

"How do they get the pieces into the *kama*?" I asked. "The pieces are so big and heavy!"

"A coal truck drives up to the house, puts a chute from the truck into the street, then into our alleyway and then through the window opening that leads into the *kama* and then the workers shovel the coal in its place."

"Wow," I said. "Isn't that hard to do?"

"That's part of their job," he replied.

It made me feel good to know what the thunder had been, that the night noises had been my Dad, and not evil spirits. Later on, I learned in school that the coal my father used was called anthracite, a hard coal with a bluish tint.

My father showed me how he lit the furnace using kindling and the old newspapers he used to read, called *Der Tog* in Yiddish or *The Day* in English. I watched him scoop up the coal with his shovel and pitch it into the furnace. I saw his physical strength as he strained while feeding the oversized kiln. The work was very hard, the coal was heavy and dirty. When my father finished, he was covered in coal dust all over the oldest clothes that he owned. My mother wanted him to share this arduous work with his older brother, but my father refused to consider it, and defended his work, remembering the original agreement he had made with his brother who provided him with his ticket to come to Amerika.

There were two other *kamas*. One was designated as storage for the family's Passover dishes, pots, pans, silverware and glassware that were individually wrapped in old newspapers every year and put into heavy barrels. My father carried all these items down into the cellar and lifted them onto shelves, although still supervised by my mother, the acting general in command.

The other *kama* was the most mystifying of all. It housed my father's old wine press, two large barrels, alcohol, large rocks and other mysterious items and devices such as corkscrews, empty bottles, strainers, jars and cans. This was where he concocted his famous colorless and odorless home brew, a 150 proof white beverage made from blueberry grapes that my mother would pick during the summer seasons in the Catskill Mountains. She called them *yagdebs*.

It is in this room, in this *kama*, that he continued being a true "vintner," a winemaker. Quite possibly, the family name of "Winter" may have come from this association.

My mother's only invasion into the darkened cellar was when she used an old, but useable oven near the coal heap. There she would cook the most wonderfully brown seasoned roasted chicken in a large brown grocery paper bag on Friday afternoons for the forthcoming Sabbath. The fowl that she cooked and her chicken soup were beyond gourmet.

She would store empty glass jars along with miscellaneous and mismatched covers in our kitchen cabinets. Jars of soup were given to family members and friends as a major treat because the soup was in great demand. She refused to store the jars in the basement due to all the coal dust and dirt that gathered there. Because most of the jar covers did not snugly fit, she would incessantly curse in Yiddish until she got one to fit. When that failed, she devised a way to close the jars by ripping wax paper, placing it over the top of the jar and securing it with rubber bands, making a tight seal. Moments such as these were comic relief in the serious-minded household where our family lived.

Rarely did my father have the leisure time to sit on the raised porch on the front of our house that he had built by a contractor. When he did find time once in a great while on a Sunday, I pestered him to play games with me.

I had found a red Spalding ball in the street one day and used it to play stoopball by myself on our outdoor house steps. Games such as boxball, or three penny boxball were popular games of choice in that day. "Pitch the penny at a marked line" was yet another game played, with the challenge being to toss the penny as close to the line as possible. Because I wanted my father to play with me, I asked him to play hit the penny, the game that I thought was the easiest for him. All we had to do was hit a penny on the ground from an equidistant spot with the ball. Whoever hit it ten times first would be the winner.

On that particular Sunday afternoon, my father was exhausted from a week's work and sat nodding off in a porch chair. When he was somewhat awake I asked him to play. He said, "I'm tired and really don't feel like playing."

I said, "You can sit in your chair and play from there!" Not wanting to hurt my feelings, he said "ok."

I realized that his heart wasn't in the game and that he was uninterested, really quite tired and bored. The game quickly came to an end. He said he had to take a bath and get ready for work the next day. He said that games and ball playing were *narishkiten*, foolish and a waste of time.

He had been conditioned to accept the notion that in America "time was money." He lived his life in America by accepting that code. The only real relaxation that my father enjoyed was his weekly bath on Sunday afternoons. In his mind, this had to be his reward for the toil he experienced each week of his life. It became precious time for him to purge himself of the sweat, dirt, tension and toxicity of the rigors of travel and heavy workload that he bore. This was the way he recharged his batteries for the beginning of the next work week.

The bathroom was proclaimed off-limits to my sister and I on Sunday afternoons. For my Dadee, the bathroom became a *shvits*, or steam room, his own personal Roman bath where he cleansed his body. He engaged in filling our white porcelain tub with almost boiling hot water, so hot as to where he could just about stand it, water that steamed the bathroom into a foggy landscape. The water level reached his chin and sometimes beyond. His skin turned pinkish red, as if he was burned by the sun.

I would peek into the bathroom, through the slightly ajar and unlocked door. This provided about an inch for air to escape, but more importantly, it allowed me to bend down on my knees to peek inside. I could see my father enjoying and relaxing himself, as if he were sitting on a throne, like a king submerged in water. I would see him pulling the plug to let the cooler water drain out of the tub and then pour more hot water into his vessel. The color of the water in the tub changed from clear and white, to light grey, to dark grey and ultimately to black, leaving a ring around the entire tub.

Sometimes my mother would actually ask me to look in on my father, because she was fearful that he was prone to nodding off in the tub and might cause himself injury or even drown. Eventually, she trusted me enough to bring him a large bath towel when he was done bathing. Seeing my father naked, not having a single hair on his milk white body, except for his light blonde pubic hair was an incredible sight for a young pre-school child to behold. My inquiring nature prompted me to ask him many questions about male anatomy. These memorable bathroom experiences became my coming of age lessons in sex. I was a curious and wanting child, eager to know about my masculinity. This was the beginning of my maturation as a young male.

As a young child, I never usually got mad at my father for any legitimate reason. However, sometimes I would feel frustrated at him because he was rarely home due to his work schedule. When I entered elementary school I was placed in a class with students whose fathers were also work beasts. Once acknowledging other kids having the same problem, I began to accept the reality that my father's workload was necessary for him to make his livelihood.

My Dad, who was a devout Zionist, was also involved with philanthropy and securing money for the new state of Israel after WWII. I felt neglected as a child because of this. Once, I said to him in anger, "Israel is really your son, not me."

He couldn't answer me right away and tears welled up in his eyes, pouring down his cheeks. He was very emotionally hurt, and felt guilty, not realizing that I was affected in that way. It was a difficult moment for both of us. Later he explained why he did what he did, explaining what happened to his family in Poland because of the Holocaust. I then understood the situation and better recognized that I was somewhat selfish wanting his attention for myself. The issue about his charities and Israel was never brought up again.

A big turning point came about years later, when as a grown, married man I earned my Master's Degree from Brooklyn College. My parents had never attended or had been part of any involvement in my educational life since elementary school. My mother had always been self-conscious, embarrassed, intimidated and afraid of that social interaction and my father was equally and conveniently always consumed with work.

I told my father, point blank, that if he did not attend my graduation from graduate school and went to work instead, I would never speak to him again in my life. He came. Maybe, just maybe, at that point in time I started to become Sam's Son.

Another incident that irked me this time involving my mother was her trying to get her way by faking yet another epileptic seizure. I was twenty years old, and had already been thinking about leaving home and going out on my own. In front of my parents I packed a bag and told my mother that I would not, like my father, tolerate her attention seeking behavior anymore. I walked out of the house, saying that I would never return.

Apparently, my mother sobered up quickly and immediately begged my father to run after me and get me to come back home. He literally ran out of the house, stopped me halfway down the block and begged me to return, claiming that from then on, things would be different. I still said, "no."

But then he said, "I never ask you about anything you do. Please. I ask you now, come back. Do it for me."

I couldn't say no to him again. This time I was returning home for him alone. I felt that I owed him that much. My mother never again concocted another fit or seizure in our house.

Although my mother outwardly ran the show in our house, my father's decisions were the final word in most situations. He was the wise, bright and intelligent force in our home. He was the decision maker, respected by a multitude of people in his world, especially my mother. He became my mother's judge.

I believe that he felt that he had the power of purpose within him to give to others. He had been lucky to come to America, escaping the Holocaust. He had a moral and practical sense about how to do good and honor the tenets of morality and the codes of the Ten Commandments and their spiritual values, although inwardly he deplored the dogmatic and ritualistic traditions of Judaism. However, he never demeaned the faith.

He was a man of few words by choice. He did not make his mark by Kant or rhetoric, but by his actions derived from his inner worth, his heart, his eyes and his feelings. His philanthropy motivated from his soul, his *neshomeh*, to his family and the state of Israel became the building blocks in his life. In the practical sense he was an air raid warden during World War II on the block where we lived in Brooklyn, a union man and a *landsman*, a compatriot to his old friends, and a fervent champion of the downtrodden.

He was a peaceful person where virtues came from empathy, deeds, commitment and charity that he felt for others. Being his son was to be exposed to a world where he was the sunshine beaming on me, showing me a pathway of reason, purpose and direction that I might explore in my life. In a way, he helped me discover myself by providing a glad hand to others.

I selected the noble profession of teaching, imparting knowledge to those in need, not necessarily for money or self aggrandizement. I taught to provide the empathy, philosophy, skills and understanding necessary for others to improve their lot in life.

My father, by his presence alone, was the silent communicator. As if almost by osmosis, I could feel and knew what he expected of me. I was not showered with material worth, but rather I was afforded with quality time with my dad, when he was present, as a result of his philosophic purpose and compassion for others. I learned from his experiences in life and how he acted, adapted and operated in real time with real people in real life situations. He became a model for my own behavior.

He never really said, "I love you" to me or anyone else in those exact words. However, you could feel his expressions of love in his sensitive eyes when he looked at you. It was warm and implicit.

In writing "Becky's Boy" and "Sam's Son," my intention was not to create competition between my mother, who called me "her boy," and my father, who called me "his son." Rather, these anecdotes deal with the perceptions that we all had of each other.

Early in my life, as young immature child I saw negativity in our immediate family. As an adolescent I saw the warts, quirks, neurosis, fears, anxieties, imperfections and basic dysfunction within our home.

Despite what appeared to be the misconstrued incompatibility of my parent's relationship as I envisioned it then, in retrospect I realize them to be a force with a wholesome bond forged together in acting as a team, but each having their own identity.

I have come to recognize their commitment not only to each other, but also to see their growth as a couple built on the principles of trust, dependency, obligation and convenience. They further grew as a partnership and learned to accept the matrix of marriage to love one another not necessarily in a physical or sexual sense, but in a spiritual and cerebral way. Their acceptance of marriage vows was consummated with children who became sacred to them as part of a family satisfying the human condition.

They adapted and resigned themselves to the mores and conventions of a new society and environment in America, in order to survive and endure in a foreign land as a wholesome unit.

It became quite apparent from their exposure to anti-Semitism, the depression of 1929 and the Holocaust of World

War II that they had found resolve, purpose, and meaning in their lives, beyond family, not only to be in some way part of this country, but also to be Zionist sympathizers in their thinking and deeds concerning the state of Israel.

I can only rationalize from my life experience now as an adult, that what I perceived as a dysfunctional family as a youngster was quite the norm, and not the exception in the world.

With respect to my parents, I can only presuppose how they perceived their only son by how I was referenced by them with different names. My mother saw me always as a child who should always be obedient, even as an adult, to be seen and not heard. My father became more accepting in his later years as I matured and came of age. He now approved of my accomplishments as a father and proudly called me his son.

I, on the other hand, always saw my Dadee as a good Sam and father.

Now, in the twilight of my life when I think of my mother, I think of myself as her boy. That feeling alone makes me feel good, and young once again.

The Glove

As a kid growing up I always knew my place. Because I was sickly and often depressed, I pretty much never asked for any material things of consequence from anyone. I would have been content just being healthy, for any short period of time, or even to be able to eat without having to endure severe cramps from stomach pains. I just wanted to be a normal child.

Because I was short and thin, I would often feel out of sorts whenever I was sick. I couldn't digest my food properly and frequently vomited—my mother constantly attempted to buy different foods in hopes of helping me feel better. In spite of her best attempts, nothing worked.

Therefore, I learned to accept my lot of being miserable in my young life, experiencing much pain and suffering until my undetected, infected appendix was finally removed. The operation became, in retrospect, a great turning point in my life—I believed I was going to die and said goodbye to my parents.

Having awakened and survived the haloed experience, I thanked my parents saying, "I will never forget what you did for me." Their response was to say nothing, but to kiss me and cry together. It was a moving experience, seeing my mother, a non-crying person, and my father, who always shed tears, both crying together, expressing their joy and happiness.

I felt as if I had been resurrected with a new life and given a new chance, that I had received a gift from G-d to continue living. It was after they left the hospital room that I made a silent promise to myself. I promised to do everything in my power to get strong and never be sick again. I willed myself to be well and be as good as possible in everything I would do and experience for the rest of my life.

It was quite a tall order for a pre-teen boy coming from nowhere to want everything that could possibly be attained in life. This promise became the foundation for my rebirth. It was up to me to move forward into the real world, build upon it and apply myself, always remembering the solitary, unrewarding and unproductive, sickly world from where I came.

In that unsatisfying world, I have no real recollection of having received toys or gifts as a pre-kindergarten child. Instead, my mother once gave me an empty cardboard Quaker Oats canister and a large cereal spoon to play with. She was afraid that I would bend the spoon, so she replaced it with a large wooden ladle, which incidentally gave me a better sound when I banged it against the cardboard canister.

My mother also encouraged my father to give me an old, sticky deck of pinochle cards. The cards were so sticky I had to treat them with talcum powder to use them. Later on in life my sister would loan me her Monopoly set, which I would play by myself.

Those items represented the sum total of my childhood possessions to go along with my poor self-image. I felt as if I was little more than a deprived child with no self worth.

Because of these feelings in my young life I always rooted for the underdog, the small guy, the weakling and for those persons least expected to succeed. For example, this was the case with Pee Wee Reese, also known as "The Little Colonel," the Brooklyn Dodger captain and short stop who became my idol. It was only later on in life I found out that Pee Wee Reese was not a pee wee at all—he was close to six feet tall and was given that nickname when he was younger. He was still my hero and always someone I looked up to.

When I returned home from the hospital to my "new world," I worked up enough nerve to ask my father for what became my very first possession in my young life—a Pee Wee Reese model baseball fielding glove.

The moment of truth did not come easily for me. It was, in fact, quite a worrisome experience. At first I was afraid of asking my father for the money. He was quite frugal, always remembering the 1929 depression. Furthermore, he did not follow sports or think it was important or relative to life. I was fearful that he might say no to me, rejecting my plea, thus causing me to become depressed and feel like a failure. My ego would be shattered, as well as my confidence, perhaps because I felt I might not even deserve the glove. The fear of failing was appalling to me. I even put it in my mind that I would beg and plead for the glove if necessary.

Luckily, I never had to do this. He bought me the glove, Pee Wee's glove. I felt I had made a connection with Pee Wee though the glove, and proudly wore it on my left hand when I played ball. I would wish somehow, some way, that one day I would be as successful as Pee Wee was. It was truly a great thought, but ultimately a unrealistic dream.

My next door neighbor Morty, on the other hand, who was about 2 years older than I, had bought the very finest baseball glove anyone could buy. It was an expensive, high-quality four finger soft leather, broken-in combination fielder and first base-man's mitt with a large oil treated pocket. It happened to be the most magnificent glove I had ever seen and really wanted, but could never afford, without a question in my mind. Of course, I could never dream of asking my father to purchase this glove for me. Therefore, I learned to be flexible and compromise. I also realized that I wanted to be true to Pee Wee, and was completely happy with the glove my Dad purchased for me.

The glove was the beginning of my coming into the real world. I had finally received permission from my parents to leave the block where I lived to go with Morty to the adjacent park to play baseball.

Welcome to the real world. Morty was tall, strong and athletic. He could hit the ball a country mile. He, and those like him, monopolized hitting the ball, while the smaller and thinner built others, including myself, would be left to languish on the field, never getting a turn to bat. We only got to field the ball should it happen to fly in our direction. Most of the smaller guys felt inadequate, but the lesson we all learned was that one day we would be bigger and stronger, that we had to be patient and wait our turn. In the meantime, we worked out and built up our little bodies the best we could to prepare for that day's arrival.

For me, that time did come. I gained weight, grew in size, stature and strength and became twice as competitive as I had ever imagined I could possibly be.

One day while in junior high school a few years later, some of my friends began referring to me as "the high-stepping Winter." It was then that I knew that I had arrived. Although the remark might have been said in a derogatory manner, referencing Hitler's high stepping marching soldiers strutting along with the Nazi sponsored goosestep, I took it as a good connotation, as a personal commentary of how aggressive and combative I had become in sports. It was validation of the promise I had made to myself in the hospital when I believed that G-d had given me another chance to make my life good and strong.

The glove, my very first possession that I ever really openly wanted and secured, will always be remembered because it gave me the control, the power and the ownership needed for my psyche to excel in my world. It became my springboard for me to flourish in life. The glove became the trigger and key not only for survival, but also to instill in me the wherewithal to prosper in a very competitive and sometimes unfriendly world. It tested my mettle as a person, to examine myself as I faced my own maturation as a growing youth.

The Jacket

A jacket is nothing more than a protective outer garment worn by humans. Through the passing of time it has assumed many manifestations. Dwight D. Eisenhower, a respected general and hero of World War II, had a memorable brown belted jacket named for him that he proudly wore in military service.

Jawaharlal Nehru, the first prime minister of the Republic of India, was clothed in a jacket named for him, which unusually had no collar at all. A green sport jacket, a blazer, is awarded to the winner of the PGA Golf tournament played in Augusta, Georgia. Uniformed jackets of all kinds are commonplace throughout the world, and often are adorned with medals, ribbons, patches and pins.

Straight jackets are used to constrain people who might hurt themselves or others. In the Orthodox Jewish faith, a jacket-like garment called a shroud is used to bury the deceased. The most absurd jacket, however, would be the jacket worn in the fictional tale of the Emperor's New Clothes.

All of these are unique examples, each having their own specific meanings and implications to a multitude of different people. But for me, there was only one jacket in my entire life that had great symbolic significance.

It is only in retrospect that I became aware of the anecdote surrounding one particular jacket, a jacket that defined me as a person for the rest of my life.

It all began on an early spring day, frosty and chilly, in the year 2008, with winter winds still lingering in the air. I decided to defy the weather and venture to partake in my normal morning walk through the woods adjacent to my home. However, on this day it would be quite different.

Still feeling groggy in the early morning and not yet completely awake, I inadvertently stuck my hand in my overstuffed foyer closet and pulled out a jacket I had never bothered to wear, or had even seen for that matter. Startled, I thought, "What is this?"

The forest green mystery jacket with the white quilted lining had actually belonged to my son. It was his high school varsity jacket, from when he ran track for East Brunswick High School. There it had remained for years, untouched even while he lived with me and went to law school.

In my curiosity I tried on the jacket, which fit like a glove on a hand around my body. It was then, while wearing his jacket, that I recollected the story of my own jacket which I wore during my years in junior high school.

As a young kid growing up, I was consumed with sports activities of so many varieties that I seemed to be adhering to a sports religion of sorts. I, like my peers, was addicted to the point of obsession and compulsion, not only as a participant, but as a spectator too. My friends and I looked for competitions to compete in, pick up sports games of any kind in the park and fought to achieve awards in our gym classes.

When I entered the 7th grade, I was one of about 15 males that came from three different elementary schools. I quickly became friends with Jimmy, a boy who lived a block away from where I lived.

He was bright, intelligent, handsome and exceedingly talented as an athlete and student. He was an extrovert who showed leadership and organizational skills in forming an athletic and social basketball team to play in the midget league at the JCH, the Jewish Community House of Bensonhurst in Brooklyn.

Jimmy had convinced his older brother Dominick to coach our basketball team called The Knights. The players selected were primarily from our 7th grade class and friends that Jimmy knew from within our neighborhood. They were chosen based on their ability, compatibility and athletic prowess. After registering our team at 'The J', the only things that were missing from the team were uniforms and matching jackets.

Our uniform consisted of simple blue cloth tee shirts and matching blue satin shorts with the word "knights" spelled out in white lettering on our jerseys.

However, the jacket we wore was, in my mind, a work of art. It was a reversible, medium-weight, all-purpose jacket. One side featured white satin material emblazoned with a blue logo of a knight on the back, and blue snap buttons on the front. The other side of the jacket consisted of a heavier blue cloth with white letters that spelled "Knights" and white snap buttons. It wasn't only beautiful, it was functional. It would become the best thing I ever wore and owned at that point in my life.

The team had no sponsors. Most of our players' fathers were blue collar or no collar men, barely making a living in America and it was upon us to raise the money for our uniforms, especially the jackets.

Raising the money was a big challenge. Raffle books were printed and distributed to us in order to raise the funds. At that time, I was oblivious to what a raffle was or what I was supposed to do. The tickets sold at ten cents a piece, or three for twenty-five cents. It became a project, a serious means to an end. It was an opportunity to get out of my insulated house and become a young salesman with the purpose and justification to ask relatives and strangers to help our cause. I became a responsible person who could collect, manage, keep records and reach a worthwhile goal.

However, no matter what I did to raise the money it just wasn't enough to pay for everything. Somehow, some way, I had to do better. I asked myself, "what I could do?."

My next door neighbor and best friend, Jackie, was also on our team, primarily as a social member. He would have loved to play, but his basketball abilities were limited because of his poor vision. He told me that he was working at the JCH on Sunday mornings from 9 a.m. until noon as a pin setter for the bowling leagues. He asked me if I wanted to work with him because the JCH needed more pin boys.

"What does a pin boy do?" I asked.

"You could do it. It's fun and you would like it. Besides, you'd make some money," he said, and explained that the job entailed picking up regular bowling pins called "ten pins."

It sounded good to me. I asked my parents for permission, which they gave me, especially after I told them about my goal of earning money for the jacket.

I was excited on that early Sunday morning of bowling at the "J." The women's league started the day by striking duck pins, a smaller version of the regular pins, that had a rubber piece circling the entire pin around the middle. The children came next, bowling with barrel pins that were similar to ducks but were cut off at the top. Both the women and the kids used smaller bowling balls that could be cupped in the palm of their little hands.

At 10 a.m. the men's club bowled for two consecutive hours. Although the work was considered hard labor, we enjoyed the working experience, which garnered great benefits for ourselves, including a way to help us build our bodies. We received ten cents a line as payment for every game played, in addition to tips we received at the end of the Sunday morning bowling sessions. The tips were usually given as change thrown demeaningly down the alleyway. We gingerly walked down the alleys in our stocking feet to bend down and pick up the loose change. Rarely did we receive dollar bills after the three hours of backbreaking work.

Sometimes the patrons blamed us for being to slow at picking up the pins. They would often disregard the ethics of the game and quickly bowl out of their own frustration, not caring if we got hit by stray, flying pins. This sort of behavior did not sit well with us, but we persevered despite these indignities.

The money we earned helped us feel independent as young boys. We could buy sodas, eat ice cream and do anything we wanted with the few dollars in change that we received. More importantly, I felt self sufficient and grown up being able to save money for my jacket. We felt totally free and uninhibited as a result of the toils of our exploited labor, sweating away, singing, cursing and enjoying every moment having fun and working together as a team. The noise of the bowling balls striking pins drowned out our histrionics in the pits, which became our home away from home every Sunday morning. We formed a genuine, long lasting bond and likened ourselves as blood brothers, sharing just about everything at that point in our young lives.

Adjacent to the bowling alleys on the ground level of the building were the three pool tables and one billiards table. A short, stocky, bald, older man named Goody, or Mr. Goodman, was in charge of the operation. Ironically, his character seemed anything but good to us. He was rather strict, snobby, unfriendly and looked down upon us as the hired-hands, the cheap Jewish labor who just picked up pins. The only perk he allowed was to let us to play pool, free of charge, when it was slow. I often wondered why Jackie and I were disliked by Mr. G. He had never even met us before working at 'The J', and he too was Jewish, so why was he so pissed off at us?

One night, I asked my father about 'The J', one of the most respected institutions in our neighborhood. I asked, "why didn't we attend services there on the Jewish holidays when it was only two blocks away from where we lived? Why did we have to walk a mile and a half to Zaida's *shul*?" He explained, "We had to attend my maternal grandfather Max's temple as respect to my mother and her family."

Being a teenager, I was not satisfied. It still did not make sense to me.

My father responded, in Yiddish, "It's not for our Jews."

Still befuddled, I retorted, "I don't understand."

"'The J' was elitist. Rich Jews belonged there—doctors, dentists, lawyers, bankers, and professionals—successful business people. Not people like ourselves," he said. "They pay member-ship dues to belong there and give big money in donations to support the building. We can't afford going there. That's why."

I realized the stark reality of class stratification within our own faith. Then, everything made sense. In public bowling alleys in our neighborhood, pin setters were called pin boys. Many blacks, lower class whites, under-aged youths, old-timers and addicts were "allowed" to perform these menial tasks, in a time when there were no such things as automatic pin setters.

Mr. G had looked at us as stereotypical, lower-class boys, based on the nature of what we did as pin boys. Therefore, we fulfilled that niche in his life that required such prejudice and discrimination based on the expectations of those times.

Although the task was difficult, we knew what was impor-tant to us as boys—as a team—to work through it and raise the money necessary to achieve our goal.

Once we all collected the funds for our team uniforms, we were custom fitted by a tailor who took our measurements in a sports store which specialized in team uniforms and jackets in all sports. The jackets and uniforms were, quite literally, the material rewards for our labor.

At that time it was the most important thing I had accom-plished in this world. Buying my first garment on my very own was a very special and big deal for me. I loved and honored what I had achieved in my quest by acquiring this treasure. I wore the jacket constantly, day and evening, with a feeling of distinction and delight.

The team was mostly comprised of students of the Jewish faith, except for Jimmy and Dominick, who were Italian Roman

Catholics. I lived on 76th Street, while they lived on 77th. I was the son of a tailor; Jimmy and Dominick were the sons of a janitor who had a severe heart condition. Due to their father's illness, they would do their father's difficult winter season task of stoking the furnaces to help pay the rent and put food on the table. It was honorable work. It showed their considerable dedication and commitment to their family. Our team greatly respected their work ethic.

Our team was well crafted, a hodge-podge of hard-working, complicated characters. Dominick evaluated our players based on their abilities, skill level and potential.

Gerry, our left hand shooting center, was a fearless, competitive fighter who not only scored points, but was a spirited rebounder who boxed out and out-jumped his taller opponents despite his shorter six-foot frame. I first met Gerry, a handsome, masculine guy, at our Seth Low Junior High School's after-school boxing program. Our boxing ring consisted of nothing more than a few gym mats laid side by side on the cold, hardwood floor; our equipment, two pairs of old, worn boxing gloves, nothing more. There were no referees and time was kept by the next set of waiting boxers.

We were usually paired by size and weight. I had done quite well fighting kids my own height and weight. I bobbed and weaved and mimicked professional boxers from studying motion pictures. I stood sideways, had fast hands and shifty footwork. I defended against punches very well by keeping my hands high and by constantly moving—holding my own with one exception—Gerry.

It seemed an obvious mismatch on the part of the gym

teacher, who pitted the winners of each category against one another in the gym. Gerry was taller and heavier than I. But, we were the only two left and I didn't complain, believing I would still prevail. However, he wasn't only bigger than me; he was a southpaw, a dreaded lefty, who fought in an unorthodox style with a long reach, using an open thumb right hand jab.

We fought well; he bloodied my nose several times; this was the first and the last time I ever bled in a fight from being hit so hard. After the match we shook hands, showing a mutual respect for each other, and began a friendship that continued into our seventies. It was only after our fight that we both realized that we were both in the same official class in school.

Gerry was from Canada and had a different accent than most of the neighborhood kids, something from which he often took a lot of ribbing. He was quite sensitive despite his size, and became quite aggressively defensive as a result of his self-consciousness. He gradually became known as a fighter not to be messed with. Ira, on the other hand, was our most talented player and had a reputation of being an excellent athlete at any and every sport.

My first contact with Ira, who was also in my official class, was in our 7th grade gym class. I had never been in a real gym before, simply because we didn't have one in my previous elementary school. I looked at the gym in amazement, taking it all in, during our first gym class at Seth Low.

The gym was adorned and equipped with many basketball courts, rims, nets and a beautiful utilitarian, lacquered hardwood floor. The basketball courts did not have a single blemish on their surface. The floor glistened from the overhead lighting, and natural light came in through the ventilated windows. In addition, there were climbing ropes, chinning bars, punching bags, marked broad jumping mats, and thick, padded mats were neatly hung on hooks to be used in various physical activities.

Mr. B, our gym teacher, had established a program of having free play activities before our formal gym class was to begin.

He wanted to select athletic students as leaders, to supervise all of the athletic activities. The most popular of those was basketball. He demonstrated to the class what he wanted, asking an upper-class student to dribble the ball to the basket and shoot a layup. Many boys in our class lined up to compete, wanting to become a prestigious basketball leader.

When Ira's turn came about, I and everyone else, looked in awe as observers while he dribbled the ball first with one hand, then the other (and gracefully behind his back), using a cross-over dribble, as he streaked toward the basket full speed and elevated himself higher than anyone in the gym class to practically dunk the basketball through the net.

It was a sight to behold for our young eyes. What an exhibition! I couldn't believe his ability as a young seventh grader. Everything said about his arsenal of skills and reputation was true. I had now seen and experienced his abilities first hand as an eyewitness. It was evident to us all that Ira was light years ahead of everyone.

I was absolutely shocked when our gym teacher didn't pick Ira for the class's coveted basketball leadership position. It was as if he was in another world, completely disregarding Ira's blatant talent. It was as if Mr. B saw Ira as a no person. It became quite apparent that Mr. B did not like show offs, braggarts and conceited athletes. He was as conservative as they come as a person and as a teacher, having his own steadfast philosophical convictions.

Ira knew his own abilities. Although he may have been hurt for that brief moment, he never doubted or changed his game or demeanor, on or off the basketball court. He knew how talented he was and always built upon it, appreciating and recognizing athletes he deemed gifted similar to himself.

Our entire gym class was compelled by Mr. B to engage in all of the other gym activities, one of which was chinning, or doing pull-ups. I had never seen a chinning bar in my life. Each student in our class had to jump up to the height of the bar and then pull their body up to the point where there chin was over the bar to successfully complete one pull-up or chin.

The best athletes in our class had difficulty lifting their own body weight even once above the bar. When my turn came, I was quite nervous, never having done anything like this before. With the entire gym watching, I grabbed onto the bar. My adrenaline was pumping and my concentration was fixed by a fear of failing. I went on and on chinning as quickly as possible and frantically pumped out two, five, ten, eighteen chin-ups and more. The teacher had to force me to stop, saying, "Stop, that's enough, you've done the most in the class and you're the chinning leader."

I was amazed at what I had just accomplished. This was a rare crowning achievement for me, although I did not realize it at that moment. That experience fueled a confidence in me that I didn't have before in my young life. I went on that term to be one of the only two students to win the coveted P.A.L., Police Athletic Award, in the 7th grade. Ira and myself would not forget that first day in gym class. I respected his talent and he was exposed to my achievements and gifts, forming a natural bond between us.

Domestically, Ira's complicated life went in many directions. He encountered the very worst of family problems, tragically experiencing the pain of his father's death, committed by his dad's own hand. That trauma may have greatly contributed to his being depressed, being a loner, and not trusting many people. He became rather aloof, instinctively shying away from females by choice and searching for thrills later in life from anything such as gambling, going to the race track, card playing and shooting dice.

Almost as if it was therapeutic, Ira would endlessly play three-man basketball in the park with others. Afterward, he would practice his basketball skills with his own ball, all by his lonesome, until it got dark, and into the late evening when the park lights took effect. In the winter season, he would shovel the court free of snow in order to practice.

One day, I asked if I could "shoot around" with him, using his ball on the poorly lit court that he occupied. He said yes and we played a multitude of games, one-on-one; horse; five-three-one, and so on. He even played against me left-handed against my strong right hand.

It was then that the gambler and opportunist in him emerged. He tempted me to play various games for money by spotting me points in any and all of these games. I had developed an excellent right-handed set shot, which I could frequently make when I got into a good shooting rhythm. I naively and foolishly thought I could compete with Ira and hold my own. He easily took advantage of this one-sided opportunity. If

I missed even one shot in any of the games we played, he was so perfect in his game that he would prevail.

I had been taken for a ride, been taken advantage of big time; I should have known better than to play with a potential pro. He gave me the bait and I took it. Instead of accepting my loss, I pulled him into a heated argument about what had transpired. He had blatantly just taken my money! I felt cheated, lost my temper and wanted to fight him.

"I don't care if I get killed fighting you! All I want is one punch, one good punch at you is all I need to get even!"

Ira thought better at that moment and refused to fight—thinking that I looked crazy—or because he might have met his fearless match. He must have remembered my crazed eyes in the chin-up competition and decided to give me some of my money back.

We quietly went our own way after that dark incident until our team, the Knights, was formed a few months later. What came of this was an unspoken understanding between us from that moment on. Despite what happened, I respected and appreciated Ira because of his almost magical athletic talent, his ability to take control of a game and lead our team in his battle-like competitiveness.

Ira was a wizard, an athlete who mastered the fundamentals of a game and took it upon himself to go to the highest level. He became a thinking, creative playmaker of the first order. Using improvisational skills like those of a jazz musician or a tap dancer, he could share the ball or score at will and visualize the "gestalt," the entire basketball floor utilizing his peripheral vision as if eyes were located in the back of his head.

Besides being a fierce fighter and being potential professional material, he was the best damned player I ever played with, or against.

He made everyone on our team over-achievers, and made me break out my shell, doing things I would never normally do. I would often try to emulate his competitiveness. We would back each other up in fights, thus having an implicit bond forged in competition, resulting in our becoming respected friends.

Ira gave the impression of great strength on the basketball court, possibly to mask the paradox of being both a loner and a leader in life. For him, the court became his home away from home.

Many who played against him disliked him, claiming that his aggression was dirty, bordering on an unnecessary fierceness. As an example, he would dribble with one hand and jabbing his opponent in the ribs like a machine gun with his free hand. Ira's actions precipitated many a fight in the three years we played together as part of the Knights. In fact, in some quarters we were referred to as armored knights in our play and deeds as a result of our hardened aggression.

Jimmy was a gifted player in his own right. He was reliable, respected, smart and the quickest player on the team. He was a disciplined shooter and playmaking guard, displaying great leadership qualities, with the friendliest face in our crowd. As the Lou Gehrig of our team, he was the opposite of Ira; he had a good-natured demeanor to match his good looks, illuminated by his dimpled cheeks and grand smile. He was viewed as a gentleman on the court, as opposed to Ira's aggressiveness.

Jimmy was loved by the triplets, Arthur and Elliot, identical twins, and their fraternal brother Michael. The triplets, as we often called them, were well known throughout the neighborhood because in the mid-1930's, triplets were extremely rare in the borough of Brooklyn. Their father was a dentist and they were popular members at 'The J', although they weren't in any of our classes at Seth Low. We had played basketball with them in pickup games at the school's adjacent park. Jimmy quickly noted their appreciation and love of the game, their hustle and desire as team-oriented players to go with their unselfish natures.

The triplets lived a short distance from the park in a large, professional apartment building on Bay Parkway in Brooklyn. Their mother took a liking to Jimmy, whom she viewed as a mature gentleman, in comparison to the rest of us, whom she saw as somewhat uncivilized and uncouth adolescents. Jimmy was the only one who was allowed to call for the triplets at their home.

The triplets rarely left their house together to go to the park to play basketball. They all dressed differently. Arthur and Elliot rarely wanted to ever play on the same team in park pickup games. They would much rather, and often did, play against each other. It was in this context that their sibling rivalry became very apparent. It was in this way that they were able to establish their own identities.

Jimmy chose Arthur and Elliot to become forwards on our team. As Knights they played their hearts out, giving everything within themselves, always being ready to fight fiercely and protect one another or any of our players in any confrontation or situation that we faced.

They were so alike in stature, our opponents would often become confused about who to guard during games. To us, they had slight quirks and differences that differentiated one from the other, which became quite an asset for our team and a liability for the other teams.

Mel was our sixth man, an extroverted and likeable, but sometimes conceited, teammate. He lacked the passion of the triplets, but was a deadly breakaway lay up shooter.

As for myself, I generated a spark in the game by giving everything I had within me. I had worked hard to condition myself, to hustle, defend, box out and rebound without being afraid to mix it up with bigger and better players. I was willing to sacrifice my body in any given situation. I also developed a more than adequate one-hand set shot to help our team, giving us yet another advantage.

The end result of the talented core of this team was to go undefeated in league play, winning three basketball championships in three consecutive years. Our rewards were three thumb-sized individual medals provided by the JCH.

During the off season, our team entered the New York Daily Mirror city-wide tournament. The Daily Mirror was a popular daily newspaper which sponsored single elimination tournaments, in which the winner of our borough, Brooklyn, would move on to play at Madison Square Garden in a semi-final for the city championship. The reward for the victorious team was a gold watch for each of their players.

We did very well and proceeded to the semi-finals, playing for the Brooklyn Championship. We were disqualified over a disagreement between the two referees in the last five seconds of the game that turned into a melee between both teams.

Ira, our most aggressive player, had made a driving lay up to tie the game. The referee closest to the play blew the whistle saying that Ira had been fouled in the act of shooting. The other referee disagreed, saying that Ira charged into the defending player. They got into a fiery argument that turned into a pushing match and eventually a fist fight, not only between the two officials, but everyone. The Knights' honor and integrity were on the line. Gerry, Ira, the triplets and I were in the midst of the action. There was pushing, punching, grabbing, tackling and squaring off. Jimmy frantically ran around all of us trying to break up the fight, while Mel was no where to be seen.

The police quickly broke up the fight, and we were disqualified because the other team had been two points ahead of us at the time the foul had been called and before the ruckus occurred. If the foul called had stayed in our favor, we could have won the game because Ira was a deadly foul shooter.

But we lost, never getting to play at Madison Square Garden, but received sterling silver key chains for our efforts.

Nevertheless, we played as a team. We truly became knights, fighting as kin, as a family protecting its own members. We had an affinity for each other. Even in our loss, the event proved to be our finest hour. Despite our differences, hang-ups and insecurities in life, we came together to bond and truly become "The Knights."

The episode signaled the end of one era and the beginning of another. The team broke up when we graduated from junior high school that same year, as we all moved on to new adventures. Gerry, Ira and Jimmy all moved on to play for the Lafayette High School Junior Varsity Basketball Team as freshmen, varsity as upperclassmen and then continued on to play college basketball after high school.

For me, the sterling silver chain has actually remained in its original box, sealed as if in a time capsule. I never used it. After I received the award it rested in my closet collecting dust along with two medals from our three team championships that we won at the JCH. The other medal was lost with the passing of time. Unlike the preserved keepsake collection in the tomb of my closet, my jacket disappeared for all eternity. I had outgrown the jacket as I grew taller and gained weight. Both of the sides of the reversible jacket had been worn out from excessive wear. It was probably my mother who discarded the jacket with other clothing due to moth infestations.

It would have been nice to have the uniform and the jacket as fond memorabilia, but having the key chain and the medals in my possession was nevertheless quite meaningful. It suffices that I have the greatest memories of my youth and the love that our team members shared with one another. To call them precious memories would be an understatement. For me, it was a time never to be forgotten, of indescribable friendships and camaraderie.

As I approach my mid-seventies, I look back at that time and wonder why Jimmy had asked me to be a part of the Knight's team. Without question, there were basketball players much taller and more talented than myself at that point and it was a mystery as to why he had selected me.

I had kept in contact with Jimmy over the years and one day, on the golf course, I broached the question about way back when we were kids, going back at least 60 years. He was rather stunned by the question.

I had for years my own thoughts on the subject. Maybe he chose me due to the similarities between our blue-collar, no-collar fathers and the culture gap of our immigrant mothers and their failure to grasp the English language. Or, perhaps it was because we lived a block away from each other and were students in the same class. All of my reasons were based upon reasonable expectations of proximity and familiarity.

Jimmy's response, however, had nothing to do with my contemplative feelings. The thing that impressed Jimmy the most was my work ethic, undoubtedly passed on to me by my father. He admired my competitive nature and zealous commitment in sports to sacrifice for the team.

His commentary put tears in my eyes as I looked back, realizing that up until that moment, I had felt like an underappreciated and self-doubting person. Only now do I feel the appreciation that I actually did get, many years ago, playing with my team mates, the Knights.

Being on that team was the culmination of a wonderful dream mixed with a new reality. As I stood there feeling my son's satin, forest green jacket around me I remembered the power that my very own team jacket had instilled in me. It gave me notoriety, purpose, identity and meaning in my life that I didn't have before. The Knight jacket I had worn was a symbol that I had come of age. It made me a person, a somebody, a Winter for all seasons.

Walking *(Shpatseereen)*

My father would always relate to me, as a child, stories about how much walking he did in the old country, Russian-Poland, where he lived as a youth. This was because his small *shtetl*, or village, had no public transportation. He especially enjoyed looking at the prevailing sites. He loved walking in the woods or any other place to complete his childhood chores. He relished the challenge of the change of seasons, the fierce inclement weather, and the ever-present wind in his face.

Upon coming to the new country he began to work as a tailor doing a multitude of jobs in various geographical venues in New York City. In the Bronx he toiled over a sewing machine at the sweat shop and then worked part time at a cleaning store in Brooklyn doing assorted tailoring. He would complete this elongated work day by religiously walking home in any and every type of weather irrespective of the season. When I watched him enter the house he became for us the walking weatherman. I could tell what the outside weather was from his appearance. At times my mother would scold him for walking in the rain, snow or inclement weather. He would say, not boasting but in a factual way, that from the gait of his walk and the quick step power of his legs he could walk faster than the bus and get home in shorter time than if he had waited for public transportation.

My mother's history of walking was quite the opposite. She, being the middle and only female child of a poor peasant family, was the only one in the family who was not afforded the opportunity to have shoes due to insufficient funds. Her two brothers and everyone else in the family, including her mother and father, had shoes to wear. As a young girl she had rags wrapped around her feet that took the place of shoes. From wearing raggedy stockings or socks she had one of her toes amputated due to frostbite and constantly felt numbness in part of her foot. When she came to this country she had a difficult time getting fitted with proper shoes. There was a limited selection of shoes available to her. She often would buy special Red Cross shoes because they were more comfortable than any others. Eventually she had metal arches inserted in the shoes which were prescribed by the orthopedic doctor to help her walk. Although she liked to walk, she was limited in her mobility.

I first began to seriously walk through my own and neighboring suburban housing developments in my early sixties. However in time this became quite laborious and boring. I modified this route by constructing a new course walking in and about the forests enveloping the neighborhood where I lived. While in the forest, I began to experience nature's magical ways. These travels practically each and every day would transform me from being a type A obsessive, compulsive, stressed out person to an observant, self-imposed, captive patron of a peaceful environment where I could actually focus and concentrate to hear the sounds and see the sights of nature in all its wonderment. I began to find an inner peace with this solitude that I may have only before dreamed about prior to retirement as a result of this new beginning and venue.

Although allergic to various flora and fauna I still loved the outdoors and its variety of beautiful gifts. My favorite viewing season was autumn. Looking at the various trees and their preparation for the winter season I couldn't help but marvel at the beautiful shades of reds, yellows, browns, oranges and greens that complimented the wild purple flowers growing along the rarely used roadways. Each deciduous tree was uniquely preparing for its own hibernation by dropping its leaves in its own random manner, much unlike the tall-standing evergreens.

I felt as if I was contributing to this process by stepping on the various fallen wet and dry leaves on the ground, hearing the whooshing and crunch of my footsteps on their surfaces as they were whipped by the wind as if to say "hello" to the new winter season. The fallen leaves took on the appearance of a moveable blanket similar to grains of sand in a desert with no given destination except that of decomposition. This became the wonderful backdrop and colorful mosaic that I experienced as I traversed through the woods. I felt a part of nature during the morning chill of autumn exhaling my smoky breath, having teary eyes, a cold nose, and numb fingers. No foul weather was a determent to my observations. The key to my wellness in this endeavor was my respect for nature by being properly attired according to its seasonal cues.

This was only to be interrupted by the sights and sounds of the woods, such as the trickle of water from a drainage pipe and the mannerisms of various animals that I have come to know, look for and observe carefully. Usually once throughout the year I would see a small garter snake on the road wiggling its way home. Upon occasion, a turtle would slowly make its way to the land of wherever. Opossums would splash their way over and mostly under the water of a deep drainage ditch alongside the roadway. Squirrels busily rushing through their workday gathered nuts in many places preparing for the harsh winter.

The early dawn pecking of a woodpecker could be heard against the trunk of a tree. The arrival and departure of many birds in the spring and autumn seasons such as red robins, blue jays and the perennial black birds or crows perched atop the high tension wires leading into developments and out of the way of old houses. The overpopulated deer, usually just-born fawns, were at first not fearful or even aware of me walking in the woods. I would gaze at them and they would concurrently look back at me, transfixed in time and space. I would try to communicate and engage them by making rapid kissing noises with my lips which seemed to provide curiosity and a calming effect for them to not immediately run away. However, as I approached them, getting progressively closer to their location, they would instinctively pick themselves up and gracefully disappear into the woods. The white-tailed deer were in such abundance that on some days I would see their dead carcasses on the roadways. They had been run over by motorists after they had ventured through the developments' manicured lawns eating flower beds and foraging on the sweet grass. Not to be outdone were the vast semblance of felines living in the wild, comprised of all colors—greys, blacks and browns with spots—roaming through the forest stalking their prey, the field mice.

At the onset of my sojourn while walking through the development that I lived in, approaching the forest, I would see many of the owners who lived in my development with their pet dogs running the gamut from black Portuguese water dogs to beautiful white Bichons, and various French poodles, large, small and everything in between, including tea cup poodles. The most popular breed was the Retrievers—golden, white, chocolate, as well as the rough, wooly-coated Chesapeake Bays.

As I approached a somewhat pristine area I always looked for a very special bird that I would see but once or twice a year—the magnificent looking grey crane. It seemed that it would always appear on the same vast lawn surrounded by huge trees. It would stand straight as a bow at attention on its long pencil thin legs. As I approached the grey crane it would take a few walking steps and then majestically soar with a wingspan that was unbelievable and uniquely its own, appearing almost translucent if you looked at this wondrous creature with the sun and the blue sky in the background. For the next few days I would vigilantly look for this grey crane, but alas it was gone. I often wondered if I would see it again the next year. True to its migratory pattern, it did come back every year. Because I usually walked at the same time every day (early in the morning, at sunrise) I felt comforted that there was always a good chance I would see the grey crane again.

As I passed an individual house adjacent to the woods I noticed two pheasants always walking side by side. As I approached they began to walk more quickly and then run a short distance, disappearing into the woods. It looked to me as if they were a couple, husband and wife, but obviously I couldn't tell one sex from the other. However, this past year I saw these same two pheasants marching along with close to a dozen other little pheasants. How cute and wonderful a sight to observe. I surmise that it must have been a male and a female, hence now a grand family. They were grouped with two ducks that I always spied upon in the drainage ditch leading to a pumping station, one adorned with a green head and the other with a grey head. I would have to make the assumption that they too may also have been a pairing. During my walks at sunrise I not only heard the toot of the Amtrak train in the distance, but also the cry of the rooster as I walked by a certain house that once must have been a farm. The farmer quite possibly still kept his roosters and hen in the all but abandoned farmhouse barn.

But for me, the most interesting thing that I saw in the woods were yet another couple, not two animals, two ducks, or two pheasants, but simply two trees, two trees that I had noticed for years. What made them remarkable, interesting and special to me was that they were standing side by side off the road by the forest and that they had a character, and a purpose unto themselves. They no longer had any leaves, were practically bare at the trunk and in a state of decay. The bark of the trees had turned a combination of grey and green colors that completely coated its trunk and its branches, resembling the forms of amputated human arms.

The trees themselves almost looked like the dried, muddy, leathery skin of an elephant. With each successive month and year it became very apparent that these trees would appear to be completely dead. Undergrowth began to sprout and emerge beneath the trees growing to about three feet in height, starting to overtake the trees. But somehow the trees still prevailed. During this past winter season we had experienced some great storms in the area, and yet the trees still stood tall and regally handsome. These trees certainly were a couple, being part of the same tree family although they were about fifteen feet away from each other.

Could we, would we, say that they were completely dead, or were they in fact still alive in their own way? If they were dead, assuming ninety-nine of one hundred tree surgeons would agree with that diagnosis, why were they so magnificent and erect in their standing? What kind of tree was this? From observing these creatures of nature the trees became to me symbolic tombstones and markers from another time.

After analyzing the shedding molding bark, I ascertained that the trees once bore apple fruit. Is there a message we mortals can take from the observation of these dead, but standing trees? I believe humans can relate to the trees because aging is a natural process for all living things whether insect, flora or fauna.

Life is a process, a cycle with a beginning, middle and end, likened to a book or musical composition delineated by birth, middle age and death. Can we make valid associations with ourselves as living beings as to what happens to us when we get older, as our bodies begin to decay? Are we, in effect, dying while we are still living? As the bark of these trees begins to separate and eventually cleave from the trunks and fall to the ground exposing the nakedness of the trunk, do we as humans begin to lose our bark, literally our will to live, our physicality, our speech, our contributions to the world in which we live? As we decay how can we, like the dead and dying trees, live eternally, not in the physical sense, but in a metaphysical sense? The answer may lie in our deeds throughout life and from others' memories of ourselves.

Walking in itself is the evolutionary process from our very first steps as children to our very last for others to see and know us as a human entity with each of us leaving our own unique footprint.

Each year with the passing of time and the onset of winter, the undergrowth begins to disappear and I again see the majesty of the old apple trees. Like a Phoenix of the forest, each tree stands again, without any encroaching encumbrance or any envelopment by other plant life.

As I walk past those trees and enter the development I then begin to bump into people similar to myself who have begun to walk a similar route as I do every day. Those who I come in contact with, in the main, are couples. A woman jogger running with her dog. A tall and short Chinese couple who are ever so friendly by saying "hello" and continuing with "have a nice day" and another Chinese couple who merely gesture and wave. There are others yet, some sour pusses who jog by themselves and say nothing and look away from you as you walk towards them.

As I walk towards my house I know that I have accomplished a great deal. My lungs are full of good clean air, my feet have begun to burn as a result of walking four and a half miles, yet I feel cleansed because I have met and been with the products of nature throughout my sojourn in the woods. These products and gifts of nature have indeed become for me a walk, or as my father would say a *shpatseereen,* with the friends of the forest.

Either Something, Either Nothing
(Oder Epes, Oder Gournish)

The evening started innocently enough as two couples met on Saturday evening, agreed on a local Italian restaurant and went out together for dinner. The food, the talk, the service and the company were rich and satisfying. The conversation was spirited and refreshing and blended into the atmosphere of the restaurant. Afterwards, we went to the home of our friends for desert.

There we relaxed and listened to piano solos of Gershwin, Kern and Arlen singing along with forgotten lyrics in a haphazard way. We played the game "name that tune" as our male host, not an accomplished musician, struggled through the compositions with long pregnant pauses between each phrase.

We then broke away and coupled off, I with my male tennis companion of 40 years, and the women with each other. After much reminiscing of past tennis matches and unforgettable personalities we somehow gravitated towards speaking about our youths. My buddy recalled his childhood friends and his early school experiences which were paramount to his respect for education. As an accomplished student and PhD in mathematics he ultimately became a teaching chairman of his math department at Pace University in New York City.

I thought for a moment and recalled my early childhood experiences when I invited myself, at the age of four, to visit my father's bed and indulge in conversation every other Sunday morning. That occurred when my father didn't work a seven day week. These were great moments for me to capitalize on, before I could even read or write.

However, my ability to reason resulted in my asking a countless assortment of "why" questions relating to the sun, moon, stars, heavens, clouds, rain, snow, and just about everything and anything to satisfy my curious mind. Trying as hard as he might, my father struggled to answer my queries.

Most often he simply gave up and said, in Yiddish, "*Ich visen nisht*," meaning, "I don't know." As I continued to pursue my inquiries he would say "*Man tracht un G-t lacht*," meaning, "Man strives and plans and G-d laughs." That response stopped me dead in my tracks and absolved my father from any further prodding. It was a profound comment. Little did I know as a child that this statement would affect me so profoundly as a man.

My tennis friend and I further addressed various other topics such as diet, exercise, retirement, and how one copes with leisure time. But the topic that intrigued us the most were the advances in medical technology resulting in prolonging the lifespan of humans. We both agreed that these advances led to bringing a better quality of life to peoples' existence by developing human intelligence to become the supreme masters of all intelligent forms of life on our planet.

Our discussion then gravitated to the metaphysical as we explored the topics of death, reincarnation, the soul, the solar system, space and beyond as well as the Creator and creation of all life forms everywhere and anywhere.

In our attempt to decipher the creation we weighed the biblical narrative with its scientific interpretation. In the literal version of the Old Testament, seven days encompassed the entire creation. Many scientists gave credence to this theory by expounding upon it by saying that time itself can be measured beyond its literal meaning in the bible.

They postulated that a day, in our time measurements of today, could be a billion years old using the geological timeframe as a yardstick. They said this would agree with the Hebrew Old Testament of the Bible accepted by most of the monotheistic religions of Western societies such as Judaism, Christianity and Islam.

The concept of G-d was intermingled with the creation itself. G-d's name was as different as were the cultures of many societies who embraced the belief in this absolute faith. For others who did not accept the faith, the eternal question was, "Is there a G-d responsible for everything that is?"

Concerning the topics of reincarnation and the soul living beyond death we agreed that these beliefs were man's constructs looking to give further justification, meaning and purpose to human life. We accepted the notion of ashes to ashes and dust to dust as the resultant attained beyond death.

Scientists of all types too numerous to mention through logical reasoning, deductions and factual formulations have studied other heavenly bodies, our solar system, endless space, meteors, comets, black holes, gases, vacuums, one celled creatures, particles and atoms.

On a human level they have tinkered with the ideas relating to robotics, kinesiology, telepathy, mind reading, mind melds and DNA. We asked the following questions with each other: Is there a vacuum far beyond anything we know of? If so, is it devoid of what? If so, is that indeed empty, or is it something? We then stopped and thought about our dialogue. What were we actually thinking or saying and did it have meaning or not?

After much thought, I surprisingly chose to bring another Yiddish expression to the conversation. It was an expression that came from my mother when she was perplexed, but still opinionated: "*Oder epes, oder gournish,*" which meant, "either something, either nothing." I coupled this with my father's profound comment from earlier in our conversation which I never ever forgot: "*Man tracht un G-t lacht.*"

I came to the following conclusion: The beginning of anything or everything either comes from something or there is nothing. By definition, if there is nothing, then there has to be no creation of any kind, just nothingness. By the same token, if there is something, that something has to be looked at as a creation which must have had a start or a beginning of some kind.

Hence the creator or G-d in its abstract formulation by humans states that all things that are created are done so in a most definitive way. For example this can be seen in all matter of life such as humans, plants, insects, or anything and everything with a specific purpose in mind. Their beauty is in their logical design, their specific order, which cannot be random.

Therefore SOMETHING over nothing answers the eternal question. Is there a G-d or creator? That something from various cultures and religions of our world, known by many different names, is part of our quest for reverence, and the recognition of life itself.

We then proceeded to partake in having peach cobbler and chocolate babka.

Epilogue

Whenever I visit my parent's graves, I say prayers and place little stones as an offering atop the headstones. Then, by habit, I stop, look and walk by the graves of the inhabitants whose lives had touched my own. Within a very short distance, maybe fifty yards, I see the headstones of "the Chicken Man" and the side by side graves of my Uncle Harry and Tanta Betty.

Cast by death as characters on a grand stage, these players are anchored as monuments remaining to pay tribute to the common folk who struggled to overcome the hardships of the human condition.

The connotation of simple familiar objects and personalities took on very powerful meanings as I probed my past. These recollections, initially seen through the eyes of a four year old boy, give credence, substance and direction to my coming of age.